THE POWER OF *TURBO* PROLOG™

The Natural Language of Artificial Intelligence

THE POWER OF *TURBO* PROLOG™

The Natural Language of Artificial Intelligence

Ralph Roberts

TAB BOOKS Inc.
Blue Ridge Summit, PA 17214

FIRST EDITION
FIRST PRINTING

Library of Congress Cataloging in Publication Data

Roberts, Ralph.
The power of Turbo Prolog.

Includes index.
1. Prolog (Computer program language) 2. Turbo Prolog (Computer program) 3. Artificial intelligence.
I. Title.
QA76.73.P76R63 1986 005.13'3 86-30101
ISBN 0-8306-0782-X
ISBN 0-8306-2782-0 (pbk.)

Cover photograph courtesy of Borland International, Inc.

Contents

Acknowledgments

THE AUTHOR GRATEFULLY ACKNOWLEDGES ALL THOSE WHO helped in the preparation of this book, with special thanks to:

My mother—who provided office space, coffee, and put up with the sometime irascibility of a writer at work.

Kathleen Doler and Borland International, who graciously allowed me to quote material from the Turbo Prolog manual and patiently answered my questions.

Ron Powers, Kim Tabor, and Leslie Wenger, who believe in me.

Mark of the Unicorn's FinalWord II word processing software, which makes writing books easy!

Introduction

PROLOG IS THE COMPUTER LANGUAGE OF THE FUTURE; A NUMBER of implementations have been available for the personal computer for some years. Unfortunately, none have gained widespread use, nor are they likely to, as they are interpreters, not compilers. They are also extremely obtuse in operation.

For Prolog to succeed, a fast compiler is needed. A compiler lets the user create "stand alone" programs. To generate the support needed for success, the compiler should be from a software conglomerate with exceptional success in marketing languages, like Turbo Pascal. And what would be a better ploy than calling it *Turbo Prolog*? But only Borland could do that!

As it happens, Borland's massive campaign to sell Turbo Prolog is under way. What is Turbo Prolog and why is it so great? Quieting an advance brochure on the package gives us a good idea:

"The astonishing fact is that Borland's Turbo Prolog gives you a $4 billion value for only $99.95.

"More than 4 billion U.S. dollars have already gone into the Japanese efforts to develop a fifth-generation supercomputer.

"Prolog is probably the most powerful computer programming language ever conceived—which is perhaps why our Japanese friends chose Prolog to be their supercomputer's implementation language.

"Without being rude about their efforts, we are pleased and proud to announce that they're not even *close* to achieving the performance that

Turbo Prolog now brings to your standard IBM PC."

Prolog, as a language concept, moves us much closer to the natural language interface that computers *should be* instead of the awkward-to-communicate-with number crunchers they are now. While the very term "artificial intelligence" is greatly misunderstood by the lay person, the relational possibilities it opens up have fantastic potential. Prolog gives us a good boost along that road.

This book is structured for several levels of software users. The novice will discover how to make his or her investment worthwhile. The immediate user will find information on getting the most out of all the features, including many tips not in the instruction book. For the advanced user with a modicum of programming familiarity, the practical secrets of more esoteric use are revealed.

Chapter 1

The Quest For Artificial Intelligence

THE HUMAN BRAIN IS A WONDROUS ORGAN. IT AVERAGES ONLY about three pounds soaking wet. And "wet" truly describes it, because brain tissue has a higher percentage of water than any other part of our body.

This soggy little computer, consisting of somewhere around 100 *billion* cells, has enabled a frail organism called "Man" to reign supreme over this world. Who would have thought, in the beginning, that such a soft and squishy animal with no fangs to speak of and no claws worth mentioning would so thoroughly gain ascendancy? An animal that was blind, deaf, and devoid of the sense of smell compared to its larger and stronger competitors.

A thing called "intelligence" (being the old-fashioned natural kind) was the secret. How could a poor saber-toothed tiger, fierce and cunning as it was, compete fairly with a being that had such weird thoughts as, "There's that old saber-toothed tiger down there. I'll just stand up here on this cliff and pound it dead by throwing down all these heavy rocks." Or: "He's in that little cave and I know there's only one way out. I'll just pile all this dry brush in front of the entrance and barbecue the scudder. Smoked tiger meat, yum, yum."

Or pity the poor mastodon, rumbling along innocently in all its long-haired, elephantine glory, when suddenly the earth opens up. Dying, the beast looks up to see these mostly hairless creatures standing around their pit-trap discussing the latest recipe for mastodon burgers.

Shinnying up trees, throwing rocks, devising traps for game, taming and using fire—all these and more were tasks that the three-pound organic computer excelled at. No other species was able to remember and associate facts like Man could. It made a huge difference. In less than 100,000 years—a mere blink of an eye in the evolutionary time frame—we went from practically last place to number one seed. No other animal is currently even in contention.

EXTENDING OURSELVES

David Ritchie, in his excellent *The Binary Brain: Artificial Intelligence in the Age of Electronics,* discusses the real reason for our triumph. We succeeded against all the odds, he points out, because Man used his (and her) big brain to do such things as domesticating fire and making sophisticated tools.

Tigers shivered desperately in their lairs during the cold winters heralding the onset of this ice age or that; they didn't think to drag in dead wood and start a fire. Man did that, and sat toasty-warm in the cave until it was time to thaw out some quick-frozen saber-tooth for lunch.

Our ancestors effectively extended their reach, something we continue to do today. The carefully controlled flames at cavern mouths extended the ability of early *homo sapiens* to produce heat in times of chill. The spears and arrows soon invented made the ability to reach out and kill game animals greater.

This concept of extension continues today. Such things as radar extend our vision hundreds of miles, automobiles extend our limbs so that we can run at 55 miles per hour, and guided missiles have vastly increased our facility in projecting deadly force far beyond spears and arrows.

Overall, however, these *augmentations* to human capabilities are good. We don't grow wings, but we can fly. We don't have gills, but it is possible to breathe under water for protracted periods of time. We have walked on the face of the moon, something no other animal can even conceive of, much less do!

Not bad at all, but there are limits.

PUSHING THE NATURAL LIMIT

Back to that three-pound mass of watery, Jello-like tissue for a moment. Nature boxed herself in with us (at least for a few thousand more years of evolutionary time). There's no area for expansion. No more room at the inn.

The brain also is so fragile that, outside our heads, it can not support its own weight. Lay a naked brain down on a table and it tends to bulge and spread out, so it's protected behind a wall of bone, cushioned securely in its dark, warm nest, taking care of business and minding the

Fig. 1-1. Borland's Turbo Prolog is a fifth-generation language development system for artificial intelligence applications.

store even when we are fast asleep. All of which means that space is limited, that our cranial cavities are now pretty well filled to the max.

Yet we've already seen that Man is a tool-building animal, that we do tend to push at boundaries and devise things to extend our grasp onward and upward. Computers are one of the greatest of these, because they expand our brains.

KEEPING TRACK OF THINGS

The quest for artificial intelligence started in a fitfully lit cavern thousands of years ago.

Man's big brain brought with it an inherent problem of accounting. The now-extinct saber-toothed tiger had no possessions other than a rather nice collection of well-gnawed bones in its lair. It was not an accumulator. The human animal is. Tools, clothing, weapons, baubles, bangles, and beads—the articles piled up in the caves.

As civilization slowly evolved and became more complex, there was more and more stuff to keep track of. No other species has the horrendous inventory control problems that Man has engendered for itself. Such complexities were much more than the minds of our primitive forebears, the Cro-Magnon people in Neolithic times, were originally meant to handle. Once they ran out of fingers and toes, that was the end of it—it all degenerated into a vague concept called "many." The Einstein of those times was the guy born with six toes on each foot. He could count to 22, reaching new frontiers in higher math!

Civilization, however, demanded a good deal more sophistication in database management and information retrieval. For a barbarian king with a freshly captured palace full of gold pieces, even 22 just wouldn't cut it. The mathematician who had to stop at 20 or 22 was likely to have his head subtracted. Reading and writing was invented. Then followed the increasingly desperate quest for computational devices. Throughout history there have been men and women of vision who recognized the need to *extend* our intelligence.

THE FIRST COMPUTING METHODS

A number of early cultures developed simple computing devices. The Chinese abacus is a prime example, remaining unsurpassed in speed and accuracy of operation well into this century. This reign of several thousand years is unequaled for a specific type of computer. Certainly the IBM PC is unlikely to equal it.

The classical abacus was called the *suan pan* by the Chinese—which meant "counting" or "reckoning" board. Small beads of bone or ivory were strung on parallel bamboo runners and set into a rectangular frame. Each row of these beads corresponded to one column of written numbers. It was an incredibly powerful tool for rapidly adding and subtracting large numbers. The proficient operator could blaze along, accompanied by a flurry of tiny clicks as beads were flipped in this or that column. It was a truly astounding manual *mind extender.*

The ancient Incas of South America made their business computers out of rope. The *quipu* was a set of knotted cords similar to the cat-o'-nine-tails that old-time ship masters used to encourage recalcitrant sailors. This provided a database management system as well as rudimentary calculation.

The Romans found their calculator even closer to home—the human hand! Because of their extremely cumbersome system of numbers, Julius Caesar and his contemporaries evolved a very elaborate system of "finger" arithmetic. As David Ritchie points out (pun, as ever, intended) in *The Binary Brain*, counting on one's fingers in Imperial Rome was a sign of education rather than the opposite.

But trying to figure MCLVIII measures of wheat at VI drachmas plus 4 percent Imperial sales tax minus 1 1/2 percent for payment within 30 days was not easy. Whether on fingers or paper, it was unwieldy at best. Obviously a further extension of the human mind was needed.

Here's a surprise. Arabic numbers really came originally from India! Indian culture is often overlooked by us "moderns," but when Alexander the Great invaded India over 2000 years ago, they were already an old, highly advanced culture. They were the ones who finally turned him back, too.

Regardless, this numbering system had a big advantage over Roman numerals because of its concept of *place value*. One column stands for the ones, the next column for tens, the next for hundreds, and so on. It's simple, grammar-school stuff for us, but it rocked the literate persons of Europe back on their heels. It revolutionized calculation. Ritchie gives an interesting example. Take the problem of multiplying MMMCCCCLVII (3458) by CCCCLIX (459). Employing the "Arabic" system, pen, and paper, a mathematician could get the answer in 30 seconds or so. A Roman, waggling his fingers like a maniac, might manage it in 10 minutes.

In a few hundred years, Man came spitting and swinging out the other side of the Dark Ages. From the Renaissance down to our own time, the demand for increased abilities to calculate and keep track of things has multiplied in quantum leaps.

The expanding of frontiers was one very important impetus to this development. The fascination with the sea and the men who went down to it in ships is a case in point. As explorers ventured out of the Mediterranean "pond" into the vastness of the Atlantic, accurate navigation tables became of the utmost importance. Down through the 19th century, many thousands of men and women lost their lives because of inaccurate

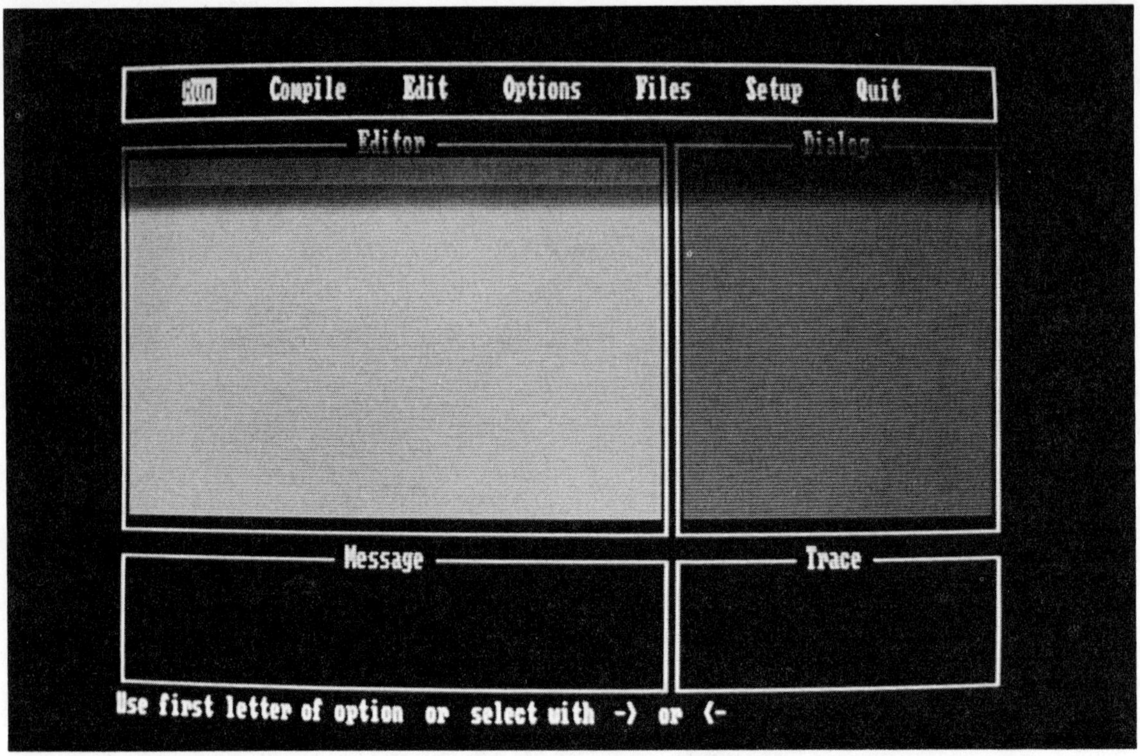

Fig. 1-2. This is where it all happens in Turbo Prolog, the main screen of the program development environment.

figures in navigation tables. Often the loud cracking of hull planking being broken as the vessel ran afoul of a storm-swept reef was the last sound many seafarers heard. A few perhaps even had the time to realize in horror that a minor error in course at the beginning of a long voyage could put them many hundreds of miles off at its finish.

Yet the sheer tediousness of the incredible mass of calculations required to construct such tables often emphasized human frailties. Attentions wandered, a number was transposed here, a decimal dropped there. Something better was needed.

CALCULATING MACHINES EXTEND THE MIND

As mathematicians roared along, expanding the boundaries of geometry, algebra, and number theories, the outcry for help became greater and greater. Isaac Newton yelled from more than pain when the apple hit his head. He realized the necessity of doing all the math to prove his theories, resulting in the development of calculus. You might say (*ahem*) that Newton fully comprehended the gravity of the situation.

The first to really achieve any success with a mechanical extension of the human brain was William Schickard, ca. 1620. He was a professor of mathematics and astronomy. Among his friends was the famous astronomer Johannes Kepler. Schickard apparently succeeded in inventing a working calculating device that could add, multiply, subtract, and divide. He planned on sending Kepler one of the machines. Unfortunately, he died of the pestilence and his workshop was destroyed by fire with the device still inside. In those unsettled times of the Thirty Years' War, his invention was lost. Had scientists gotten this working calculator in the early 17th century, there is absolutely no telling the wonders we would know today. Mankind would certainly be much farther along on the road to the stars then we now are.

Later in that century, Blaise Pascal had better, though more limited luck. A French mathematician and philosopher who had considerable impact on civilization, Pascal's greatest achievement was in the field of math called "probability theory"; he also formulated Pascal's Law, which contributes mightily to the science of hydraulics.

Like all the mathematicians who had preceded him, Pascal bemoaned the orneriness of manual calculations. Even relatively simple problems could involve hours or even days of scribbling on paper. His back ached, his eyes turned blurry, his head hurt. Worse, no one had gotten around to inventing aspirin yet.

Pascal's answer was to design a device he named the *arithmetique*, a brass box the size of a loaf of bread, with eight dials on its face that one operated by using a stylus to input numbers on the dials. By entering ones, tens, hundreds, and so forth on the proper dial, calculations up into the hundreds of thousands could be performed. Alas, the *arithmetique* was less sophisticated than Schickard's lost machine. It could only add and subtract, and was unbelievably expensive as well—so much so that one could hire a whole cart of local mathematicians to do it manually for the same price.

Some 30 years later, around the turn of the 18th century, the German mathematician Gottfried Wilhelm Leibniz had his go at it. "It is unworthy of excellent men," he is reported to have said, "to lose hours like slaves in the labor of calculation that could be safely relegated to anyone else if machines were used." His invention, the Leibniz Wheel, was more powerful than Pascal's, being able to multiply and divide as well. David Ritchie describes it as "a cross between a slide rule and an old-fashioned meat grinder." But, like Pascal's device, it was expensive and only a few wealthy dabblers were willing to pay the price for the relatively minor aid it offered. Leibniz died in 1716, ignored by his countrymen and outshone in the field of mathematics by his English rival, Sir Isaac Newton.

Yet Leibniz is really an unsung hero. His invention inspired other designers to work on calculating machines. Eventually they were refined into the computers that so wondrously fill our lives and extend our minds today.

COMPUTERS ARE BORN

Up until the dawn of the 19th century, Man's attempts to extend the mind was limited to manually operated devices. The abacus, Pascal's *arithmetique*, Leibniz's Wheel—they all required an operator who did each step in sequence. Yet the concept of *programming* was not that new. Music boxes, clocks, and various toy automata had made use of this principle for hundreds of years.

Joseph Marie Jacquard (1752-1834), a Frenchman, deserves a lot more credit than most historians afford him. He forever changed our lives by making the breakthrough which opened the doors wide to automation, computer programming, robots, and (still to come) true artificial intelligence. Jacquard gave us the means by which we *are* extending the human brain. What did he do? Just build some kind of loom, wasn't it? Spawned the Industrial Revolution and all that, didn't he? Yes, but it was *how* Jacquard did it that is having such great impact on all our lives today, whether we realize it or not.

Textile manufacturing in the 18th century was an extremely complicated, very labor-intensive process. Weavers, spending long hours hunched over their looms, tended to make many mistakes in the complex patterns that fashion called for. Jacquard saw an opportunity to get rid of this drudgery, saving money and increasing productivity at the same time. He decided it should be automated. He set out to develop a weaving machine that could be programmed to weave patterned cloth. Unlike human workers, the machine would do exactly as it was told, be completely reliable, and turn out cloth of uniform quality. He succeeded in building his automatic loom and the textile business was revolutionized.

Furthermore, it was "revolutionized" in more than one sense of the word. The workers of the early 19th century were not overly enthused about losing their jobs to automation. A series of revolts sprang up, especially in England. The English workers were called Luddites, after their mythical leader Ned Ludd. The British government put more troops in the field to quell this unrest than they did to defeat Napoleon at Waterloo. At the cost of considerable blood, the Jacquard loom was firmly established.

To interject a personal opinion here, today we are really not handling automation very much better. As in Regency times, a lot of people are losing their jobs because their vocations are no longer necessary, taken over by machines. All this needs to be planned for. A lot of retraining is necessary. The old ways cannot continue, nor will. We go on up the road, and it's a wonderful journey. Yet pity the poor Luddite: our continuing mental evolution has passed him by.

Back to Jacquard. His automatic loom worked on an ingenious principle. The steps needed to run the machine and cause it to weave cloth were encoded on cards in the form of punched holes. These were strung together into an endless belt that passed over the hooks which did that actual weaving. The holes allowed the hooks to come up and snag threads of the warp, pulling them down so that the loom shuttle would go under some and over others. This created the pattern in the cloth. The automated loom was an immediate success. It was introduced in 1805, and 10 years later there were over 10,000 in operation in Jacquard's native France alone.

Meanwhile, in England, a very odd man who turned out to be one of the most famous inventors in British history was taking note of Jacquard's invention. Charles Babbage was undeniably a genius and evidently knew it all too well. He was notorious for his eccentric and abrasive behavior. But he added a great deal of acceleration to the sea change still taking place in Man's extension of the human brain.

In 1812 Babbage came up with the idea of a "difference engine"—a mechanical calculator—and eventually secured the sponsorship of the Royal Society and the great scientist Sir Humphry Davy, a pioneer in the chemistry of gases. But it turned into a very complicated project. By 1842 the machine still had not been built and the government finally gave up on the project, withdrawing funds from it.

Babbage, however, refused to quit. In fact, he had by now elaborated his original idea into a much more complex calculator called the "analytical engine." He envisioned it as a steam-powered machine with two major parts. The first was a "mill" to perform arithmetical operations. The second was a "store" to manage variables and retain the answers to problems solved.

Babbage planned to use Jacquard's system of punched cards to run his machine. He decided to use two sets. One would instruct the device step-by-step in how to solve problems. The other set would feed variables into the "engine."

Sound familiar? It should. Here in the 19th century was Charles Babbage coming up with everything that's in the modern computer. The "mill" is the central processing unit. The "store" is the memory system, and the cards provide the means of programming.

Unfortunately Babbage died before his machine was ever built. The steam-powered technology of his time was just not up to providing the parts with the necessary exact tolerances. (In this century a small model of his machine was built as a historical curiosity and it worked.) Yet, the principles that this eccentric genius set forth made sure that working computers were just a matter of time. The brain of Man was hovering on the brink of its mightiest extension yet.

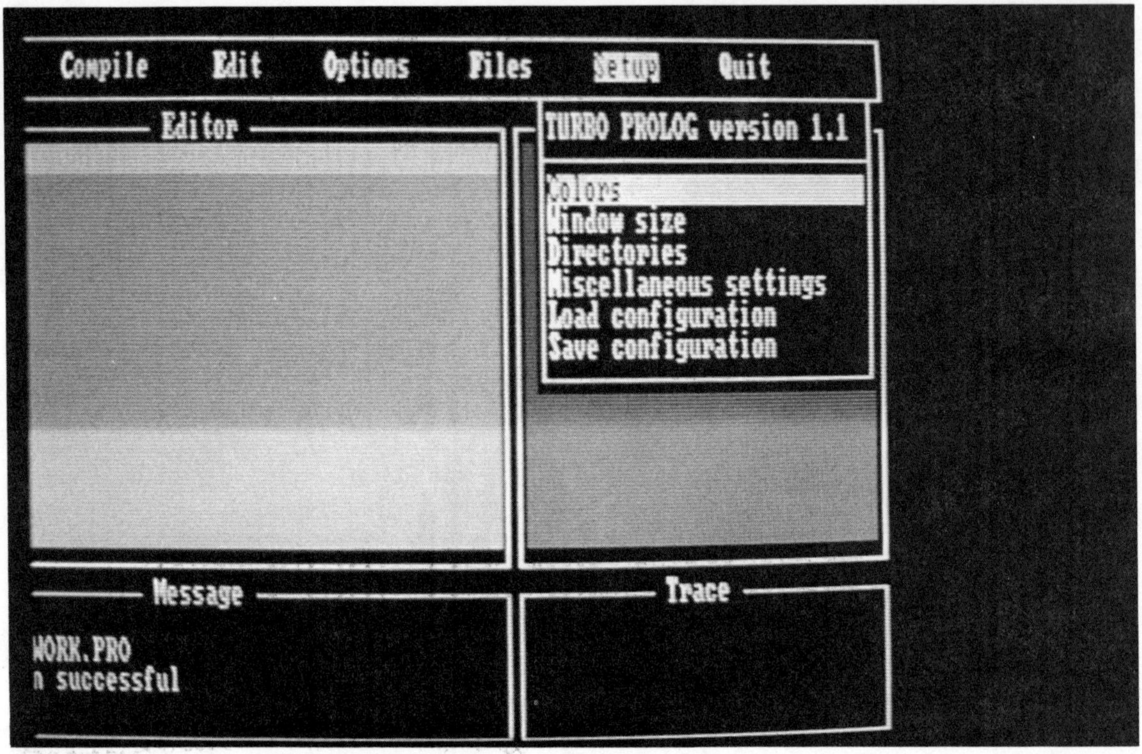

Fig. 1-3. Pull-down windows, such as the one shown here for Setup, make the Turbo Prolog environment both pleasant and efficient.

COUNTING NOSES

At last the scene shifts to the North American continent, to the lusty and brawling young nation charging full tilt toward the 20th century. But things were getting complicated. The Founding Fathers had mandated in the Constitution that a census be performed every 10 years. While originally just a nose count, the census had become much more important as the country had expanded. Such statistics as national origin, sex, number of children, and so on, were all now needed for various reasons. In 1890, however, the results of the 1880 census were actually *still* being tabulated. Obviously the job could only continue to get worse. Desperate to make some headway, the Federal government offered a prize to anyone who could supply a workable data handling system.

A German immigrant, Herman Hollerith, won it. His machine used Jacquard's punched card system. Today the punched cards like your electric bill comes on are called "Hollerith cards" in his honor.

Hollerith's main contribution was the invention of a "card puncher." Much like an old-fashioned telegraph key, information could be entered on the cards via patterns of punched holes. The punched cards could then be sent to a central location and passed through an electric tabulating machine. As each card traveled in the machine, a series of metal pins pressed gently against them. Whenever a hole was encountered in the row that a particular pin was riding, the pin would make electrical contact and send a pulse to a counter. These machines performed superbly, and the 1890 census was completed on time. Hollerith's fortune was assured. The company he founded, now expanded somewhat, is still in business. It's called "IBM."

More important, this was the first wide-scale usage of data processing. Man's ability once more was extended. Yet, a pin making electrical contact was not exactly "intelligence," artificial or otherwise. Something more was needed in the ever-growing complexity of human affairs.

Still, it was a start. Other practical ways to extend the mind were being embraced by the business community at the same time. William Burroughs (whose descendant of the same name is the well-known author of such books as *Naked Lunch*) patented a calculating machine in 1888. He had worked for a number of years as a bank clerk and was well aware of the need for a labor-saving device in accounting. Developing his machine over a period of years, his patented model was simpler and more reliable than earlier attempts.

Burroughs also founded a company which today, still bearing the Burroughs name, is one of the major computer companies in the world. For three-quarters of a century Burroughs, IBM, and (to a lesser degree) NCR were the principal manufacturers of "mind extenders" to meet business needs. Their "accounting machines " were the primary means of mechanical bookkeeping until the advent of small and affordable computers.

My own experience with these incredibly complicated but essentially reliable mechanical monsters came in the 1970s and early 1980s working for a company that serviced and sold them. Even as late as 1982 there were still many thousands of Burroughs Sensomatic accounting machines still in use, and no doubt there are still a good many.

While cheap personal computers are fast replacing the few Burroughs machines left, to a very small business based on ledger card accounting, it's very hard to beat one of these old clunkers. This is a job honed to perfection over 75 years, while software (programs) to do a similar job on an IBM PC, for example, have only been under development for the last 5 years or so. But their long and honorable service will soon be a thing of the past.

Accounting machines, adding machines, even multiplying and dividing calculating machines were nice. But the complexity of Man's endeavors had outstripped their capacities even by the turn of this century. More was needed.

LOOKING FOR A SUPER CALCULATOR

The problem with adding machines and calculators was that while they did indeed add speed and accuracy to manual manipulations of numbers, that was all they did. Each operation was performed in laborious sequence by the user. Even the carded automation of the Jacquard loom over a hundred years prior had done better than that. Even a little girl's wind-up music box was programmed to do a series of events on its own, playing tinkling trills without supervision.

A good many scientists and other thinkers in the early part of this century recognized this fact all too well. They knew these mechanical devices extended the human mind, but only in the same manner that riding in a car augments our ability to move faster and farther than a sustained jog could take us. It still took effort on the operator's part. The machines were not "intelligent" in any sense of the word. They could do nothing on their own. Worse, in the ever-growing complexity of technology and science, they were too slow. Hundreds of scientific problems especially were piling up because the necessary mathematical calculations would simply take too long even with mechanical calculators. A super calculator of some sort was being cried for from many quarters.

Professors at the Massachusetts Institute of Technology (MIT) decided to do something about it. Thus began MIT's long and continuing leadership role in the field of artificial intelligence, a role that continues today. The year 1927 saw their first major triumph. Several members of the electrical engineering facility completed development of an electronic machine that had the ability to solve simple differential equations.

Vannevar Bush was one of these professors, but he was not satisfied with the machine. Its abilities were still just too limited. Bush, as an engineer, wanted a computing device that could handle the more complicated differential equations that would be of practical use in the various disciplines of engineering. So he and his colleagues literally went back to the drawing boards.

A few years later, in 1931, their work had resulted in a more advanced machine. They called it a "differential analyzer." This device differed from its predecessor in that it was entirely mechanical. The rudimentary vacuum tube technology of the day had proved inadequate for their purposes.

David Ritchie describes the differential analyzer in his book *The Binary Brain*. He writes that it looked like a huge dishpan full of parallel steel rods. At various places gears whirled, causing the whole assemblage to "look like something from a Flash Gordon comic." Despite being something whose picture would have been right at home on the newstand—gracing the cover of a science fiction pulp like *Thrilling Wonder Stories* along with a "bug-eyed monster" and a young lady clad in little more than a space helmet—it was a *real* computer.

The differential analyzer was, unlike modern computers, an *analog* computer. In this type of machine, something is substituted for functions and numbers. This can take the form of a rotating shaft or disk, variances in electrical current, or anything else. The odometer in your car is a prime example of a simple analog computer. Here the turning of numbered drums represent mileage traveled.

But an analog computer, that is, one using these rotating shafts and gears, faces an inherent problem. As the numbers get larger, the revolutions pick up dramatically and, on very large calculations, you are apt to have whizzing shafts and blurring gears hurriedly departing your computer by punching their way through various sides of its case.

The solution these pre-World War II engineers and scientists came up with was binary arithmetic. The math we learned in school was decimal or *base-10*. Meaning we have ten fingers and ten toes and some Cro-Magnon Einstein, gnawing reflectively on a saber-tooth rabbit bone, decided it would be logical to formulate numbers in units of ten. Electrical switches, however, do not have ten fingers and/or toes. They're either "on," i.e., making connection so that an electrical current may pass through, or they're "off."

So binary or *base-2* arithmetic was the answer. Here units of 2 are used instead of units of 10, so that, converting the notation and counting in base-2, we get 0 = 0, 1 = 1, 2 = 10, 3 = 11, 4 = 100 5 = 101, 6 = 110, 7 = 111, 8 = 1000, 9 = 1001 and so on. This notation is cumbersome to humans; using it, my age is 101000 (you figure it out), or the integer 456,789 is written as 1101111100001010101. Multiplying and dividing manually in base-2 takes all fun and excitement that doing so in Roman numerals affords.

To a computer, however, as these engineers decided, this awkwardness doesn't exist. Remember the switch, either on or off? Translate that to electric pulses. If a pulse is present (its voltage and current is immaterial), then this is referred to as an *on-state*; if no pulse is present, it's an *off-state*. "On" is 1 and "Off" is 0. Thus the machine detecting "On-Off-Off-On" sees it as a 9 and acts accordingly. Even 456,789 zips right through as "On-On-Off-On-On-On . . . ," etc. This is the way your desktop computer works today. It's called *digital electonics*.

Up the street from MIT, a professor named Howard Aiken had noted Bush's success with the differential analyzer. He decided to try his hand at one using on-off electrical pulses. So Aiken took a leading role in building the first large-scale binary computer.

In conjunction with IBM (up to then primarily a manufacturer of the accounting machine pioneered by Herman Hollerith), his group at Harvard in 1938 began development of a machine that would use electrically activated relay switches instead of the whirring shafts and gears.

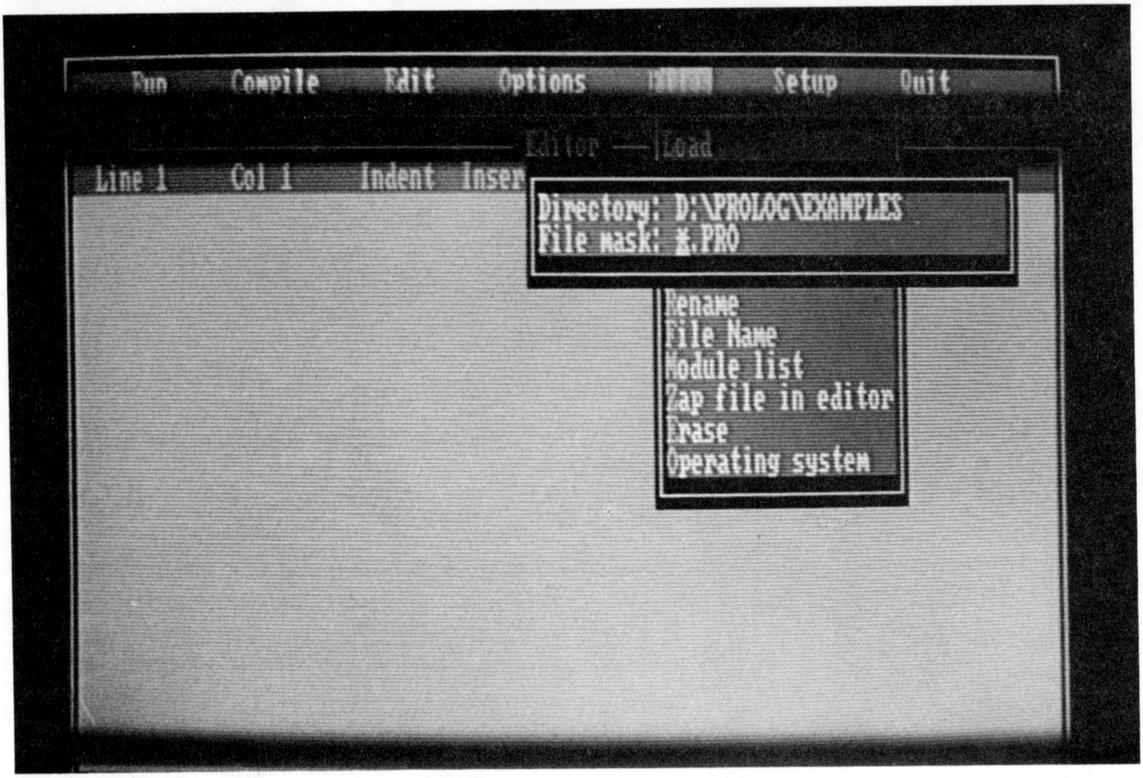

Fig. 1-4. This is part of Turbo Prolog's pull-down file management system.

A relay is a simple type of remotely activated switch; it usually has an electromagnetic coil that pulls a switch into the on position when a current passes through the coil.

BABBAGE'S DREAM REALIZED

The Harvard/IBM machine was called the Automatic Sequence-Controlled Calculator, or Mark I for short. In principle of operation, Mark I was essentially the same machine that Charles Babbage had envisioned over 100 years before. Now technology had advanced sufficiently to put his dream into reality. When steam had been unable, electricity did the job.

Mark I was huge. As Ritchie describes it, it was as "big as a PT boat and chirped like twelve exaltations of larks when operating." (An "exaltation" of larks is what a flock of those birds is called.) A newspaper writer of the time referred to the machine as faster than "twenty Einsteins."

The machine *was* faster than scores of the best human mathematicians, which may not sound like much today when we all have far more powerful computers living in little plastic boxes on our desk tops, but in the early forties it was a wonder, indeed. It was science fiction come to life!

But an engineer is never happy. As fast as Mark I was, more speed was obviously needed to handle the growing technical problems engendered by military research as World War II flamed across the planet. Electrical relays, being mostly mechanical with contacts closing to make a circuit, simply were not fast enough. Each of these openings or closings took an appreciable fraction of a second; a quicker method of switching was needed for true practical computer operating speeds.

Electronics, spurred on by military necessity and tons of government money, had improved vacuum tube technology to the point where that seemed to be the real answer. You remember tubes, don't you? Those glass things with the little red lights in them that inhabited the dark areas in the backs of radios and television sets when you were much younger? Anyway, vacuum tube switching circuits, having no moving parts, could provide the on-off states needed for binary computer operation much faster than any mechanical device. This, then, seemed to be the final solution to the next generation of computing devices.

With Army backing, a project to develop the new computer was begun at the University of Pennsylvania. The resulting vacuum tube based device was called ENIAC, short for Electronic Numerical Integrator and Calculator.

A number of engineers voiced doubt during the early stages, after all here was a monstrous collection of over 18,000 vacuum tubes. If just one or two of them blew, the whole computer could be shut down. How long would it take to find the burned-out tube? How reliable would such a device be? ENIAC proved somewhat better than that, though. Physically it was a towering device consisting of huge cabinets filled with tubes, wiring, capacitors, transformers, and all the other bulky electronic circuitry of the forties. In size, it was close to that of (as Ritchie describes it) "a fair-sized ballroom."

Sometimes this complex and incredibly power-hungry mass of metal would run for a full day or longer before a tube burned out and hordes of technicians rushed to get it running again. But ENIAC performed hundreds of computing jobs during its lifetime, including calculations used in designing the atomic and hydrogen bombs. In the late fifties—still in working order—ENIAC was honorably retired and dismantled. But a major step in the quest for artificial intelligence had been achieved. Man's brain was incredibly extended! Yet it wasn't enough. More was obviously needed.

VON NEUMANN MOVES COMPUTING INTO HIGH GEAR

The parade of computer technology—from Pascal and Schickard's rudimentary machines up to the vacuum tube monster ENIAC—pretty much follow a common pattern. Computers, in the Darwinian sense, were evolving like humans did earlier. Ritchie uses this analogy in his book also, and it's a good one. Each new generation of computing devices was picking up acquired traits and passing them along to their descendants: more computing power, better circuitry, smaller size, greater adaptability to their environment, and so forth. This continues today at an ever faster pace.

True, computers can't reproduce by themselves, at least not yet. But, otherwise this analogy fits very well and marks a very important turning point in the history of Mankind. For many thousands of years we humans have evolved in an almost random manner, subject to the external factors of environment and necessities of simple survival. It has been a long and slow process with discernible change occurring only over the space of many long generations. And it has taken equally as long a time to determine which variations are good and which are dead ends.

Now the computer has dramatically speeded up this process. Man has always been a tool-using animal, but now a *tool*—the mind-extending computer—actually is becoming part of the evolutionary forces acting constantly on us. Computers, if not yet on an individual level, are now an integral part of the species development. Take merely the last 40 years as an example in which the total sum of knowledge has increased several fold over what had taken 4000 years of history to accumulate.

To borrow a phrase from science fiction writers Larry Niven and Jerry Pournelle, this is indeed "evolution in action." The ongoing changes in computer technology in general and artificial intelligence in particular are now tied to the evolution of our species. As more and more powerful machines come on the scene and are widely assimilated, it is obvious that changes will take place, both in the way the machines are used and in Mankind itself, which will rival the original, prehistoric development of the biological brain. The Age of Information is really the Age of Brain Extension—and it's truly an exciting time to be alive!

Much of the current mushrooming growth of computer and artificial intelligence technology was made possible by one man, a Hungarian immigrant named John von Neumann, who was one of the greatest mathematicians of all time. His unassisted native intellect was so great that he was sometimes rumored to be a Martian. The U.S. government made good use of him during the infamous Manhattan Project of World War II, with von Neumann being one of the primary contributors to the creation of the atomic bomb.

Von Neumann, in the early thirties, had been one of the leading scientists and mathematicians in Germany. His various feats of calculation were already legendary, his achievements in the mathematical specialty of game theory significant. But Hitler sowed Germany's seeds of destruction by giving in to a pathological hatred of Jews. So, like Albert Einstein, von Neumann fled the Nazis and came to the U.S. The shortsightedness der Fuhrer displayed in alienating just these two men alone is astounding . Had these towering giants of mathematics stayed in the Reich, it is entirely possible that Germany would have developed the bomb (they came close as it was) and the Allies would have lost the war. Einstein and von Neumann were that important. Yet where Einstein's lasting influence was in the field of theoretical physics, with his Theory of Relativity, von Neumann's is still being felt in almost every facet of our everyday lives.

After the war, von Neumann was asked if he had given up mathematics for bombs and was just thinking about destructive devices now. "That is quite wrong," he said. "I am thinking about something a lot more important than bombs. I am thinking about computers."

But the awesome glory of radioactive fireballs blasting apart stillness of the desert dawn continued to fascinate him for some time. It may even have been the cause of his untimely death. Von Neumann was almost a fan, an aficionado of the atomic explosions he had made possible. He continued to attend many of the postwar tests and seemed to delight in them.

Atomic devices were very much his baby. He constructed the mathematical model that allowed the Manhattan Project scientists to time the triggering explosions precisely enough to effect an atomic detonation. In other words, he made bomb design orderly—just a matter of plugging the desired numbers into the proper equations. Many people faulted von Neumann for his part in unleashing this horror on civilization, but he showed few qualms, being more interested in following where science and technology led regardless of cost. This caused moral indignation in many, but it must be remembered that this genius thought on a completely different plane than most of us, with implications both good and bad. We are coming to the good, the all-pervasive, seminal influence of John von Neumann, his atonement, if you will, for the bomb.

A chance meeting in the summer of 1944 with Herman Goldstine, one of the mathematicians associated with the ENIAC computer project, introduced von Neumann to computers. He was given a tour of ENIAC and was highly impressed and fascinated. Here, at last, was the calculating device that scientists had dreamed of for centuries. A man of von Neumann's stature can do essentially whatever interests him, and computers did. He plunged into the infant science of computer technology and almost immediately revolutionized it. Like the atomic bomb, he quickly put computer science on a firm mathematical footing.

Being dissatisfied with ENIAC's capabilities, he envisioned a more powerful machine. He called this new computing device "EDVAC," an acronym for Electronic Discrete Variable Computer. In 1945 he published

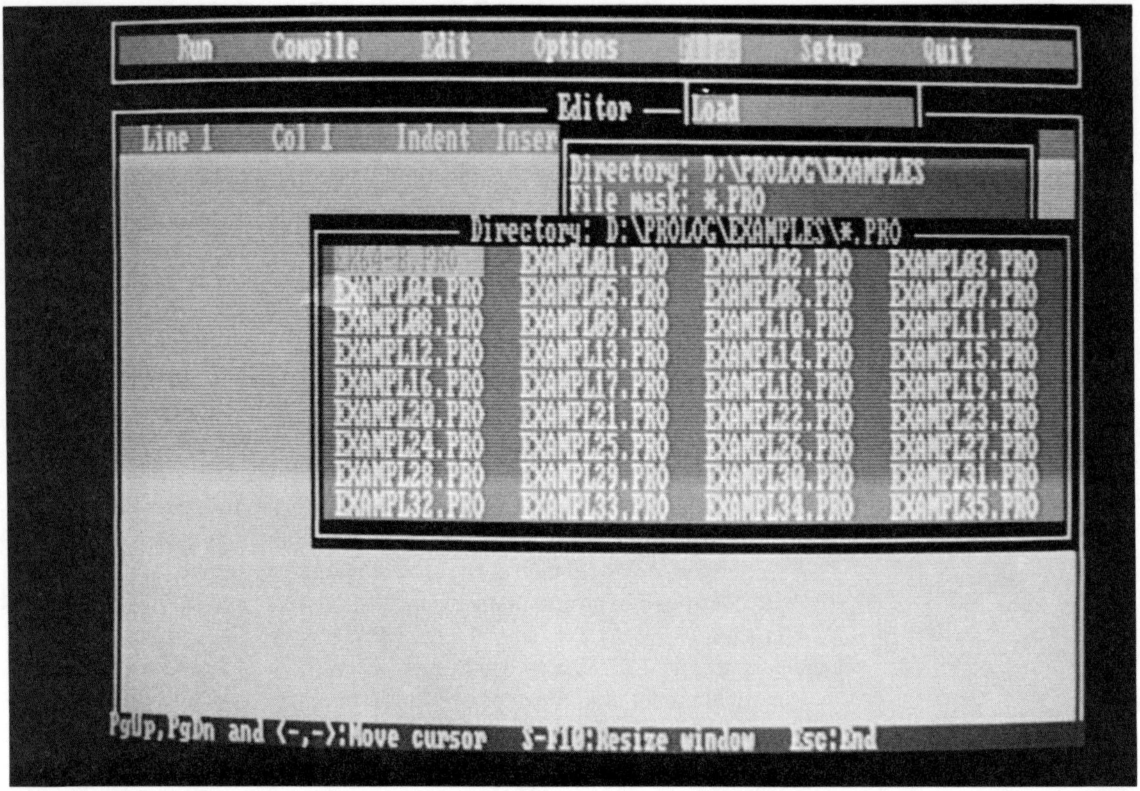

Fig. 1-5. A Turbo Prolog directory window with files listed. You may use the arrow keys to select a file and load it into the editor window.

a 101-page paper (*First Draft of a Report on the EDVAC*) describing not just that proposed computer, but in essence a logical blueprint for all the machines to follow. In fact, the many millions of computers now in existence all operate on the principles that von Neumann put forth in that report. The logical structure of how these machines process information was first detailed here.

After the war ended, with von Neumann still much in the forefront, computer science continued to accelerate. There were not many new computers built at first, each new one being a gargantuan, one-of-a-kind undertaking. Naming them became a sort of intellectual game, a chance for the dry wit of mathematical geniuses to bubble briefly to the surface. One machine was called JOHNNIAC in honor of von Neumann. Another, one he was allowed to name himself, he designated as the Mathematical Analyzer Numerical Integrator and Calculator, or MANIAC.

Von Neumann was intensely interested in finding new uses for computers. One of these was in forecasting the weather. He developed a mathematical model of the atmosphere and arranged it so that weather data could be entered and a forecast obtained. This technique is still used in computerized prognostication today.

Another von Neumann project is of even greater significance in the longer run. It was something he sometimes feared leaking to the general public, a concept science fictional in nature and fraught with controversy. Reproduction of machines by machines! Von Neumann made the assumption that all organisms were automatons, and that their operation was something that could be described via known physical laws and in mathematical terms. Mice, one-celled microbes, humans—all were self-replicating automata in his view. So he pondered what would enable an artificial mechanism to reproduce itself automatically. For a fuller explanation of this fascinating subject, I refer you again to David Ritchie's excellent book, *The Binary Brain*.

In essence, von Neumann theorized that four components were needed. The first of these is some type of automatic "factory" which would gather the necessary raw materials. It would then follow an instruction in the form of writing and blueprints from one of the other components. The raw materials would then be assembled into the specified form.

Second, there would be the "copier" to act on these written instructions and make copies of them. Third, a "control unit" must exist to act as an overseer and govern the operations of both the copier and the factory.

Last, there had to be a "master program" telling the factory how to manufacture the new assemblage. He did not detail what the proud pappy would give out in lieu of cigars, although it is amusing to speculate. "Hey, X-19, we just manufactured another kid. Here, have a floppy disk. Made in Havana!" (Not being a mathematical genius, my wit is somewhat less than dry. In fact it has been known to bring tears. But back on track.)

Remember now that this thinking about machine reproduction was all taking place in the 1950s. You can imagine the furor if the press—especially the lurid supermarket tabloids—had gotten wind of von Neumann's work: "SCIENTIST FATHERS COMPUTER." (This early, at least, none would have claimed it was a clone of Elvis or a plot by the UFO creatures.)

So von Neumann studiously avoided the press, but his research was bringing forth fruit. Having learned a lot about life as a replicating organism, now an interesting question occupied his thoughts: if life resembled mechanisms, could mechanisms imitate life? Reproduction, a moderately mindless process, had led him logically onward to thinking about the brain itself.

Now we are coming to a real milestone in the development of artificial intelligence. If a computer—being an artificial extension of our minds—theoretically could reproduce itself, could it not then go a step further and actually duplicate the functions of a living, human brain? That's the question that von Neumann was asking himself. Awesome and frightening stuff for that time, and for many people it still is today.

Remember again, please, that was all taking place in the 1950s. His conclusion that such duplication was not possible is understandable in light of the rudimentary technology of the era. Had he been so fortunate as to live a few more years, it's pretty obvious that his opinion would have changed. The wondrous explosion in microcircuitry, engendered in great part by the various manned space programs, blossomed in the late 1970s like those great mushroom clouds of atomic detonation that von Neumann was so fond of watching. Compared to the miles of wiring and thousands of vacuum tubes in his day, the fingertip-sized microprocessors of today offer incredible computing power. The artificial intelligence techniques that von Neumann could only dream of are now being realized.

As with, for example, Borland's Turbo Prolog—the prime subject of this book.

But von Neumann did not live to see much of what he had wrought. In 1955 he suffered a fall that injured his shoulder and the doctor who treated the injury found advanced bone cancer. He died just a few months later. The many atomic bomb tests von Neumann had so enthusiastically attended had exposed him to greater radiation levels than normal. It is possible that this was the true cause of his death. And we prematurely lost one of the greatest minds that ever lived. Yet his legacy in computer science lives on all around us, making all our lives better.

Ritchie, in describing von Neumann's contribution, refers to the computer as a "mental prosthesis." Computers are indeed that—an extension of the human mind, amplifying greatly our ability to retain, organize, retrieve, and analyze data. Nature took millions of years to get the human brain where it is via evolution; von Neumann and his associates accomplished the same thing in less than a generation.

That is John von Neumann's true lasting contribution, providing the means for human intelligence to make a quantum leap forward. Artificial intelligence!

THE IMPOSSIBLE MADE POSSIBLE

To have made artificial intelligence possible using the vacuum tube technology prevailing during von Neumann's lifetime would have required a monster machine approaching the size of several city blocks, requiring power enough to dim all the lights of that city whenever the machine so much as hiccuped. Practical it was not.

Technology moves on. The transistor was invented, then the integrated circuit which puts thousands of transistors and other computers on a tiny chip of silicon barely visible to the unaided eye. Huge mainframe computers are now approaching the density of the human brain. The work of such artificial intelligence pioneers as Norbert Wiener, Alan Turing, Marvin Minsky, John McCarthy, and many others is giving them incredible powers. It's truly exciting!

But the purpose of this book concerns the desktop personal computer—specifically the IBM PC and its compatibles, and the power of Turbo Prolog. A few words are in order explaining how all this power came to be available to that little plastic and metal box on the top of your desk. Then we'll move on into logic programming and begin exploring the wondrous possibilities of Borland's Turbo Prolog programming environment.

First, however, the revolution, because that's what it is.

Here we should take a look at exactly what a personal computer is and why it is or will be affecting all our lives so much. The word *microcomputer* is a generalized term now applied to almost any small computer. These computers are also called *desktop, home*, and *personal computers*. You'll hear these and other terms used interchangeably. Regardless of name, a microcomputer is simply a computer built around a microprocessor.

A microprocessor is a tiny electronic component roughly the size of your thumb. A flat rectangle with a row of electrical connections along each of the two long sides, it looks like nothing so much as some science fiction artist's concept of a robotic centipede. This small but exceptionally powerful device is a direct result of the technology spin-off from NASA's Apollo moon landing and other space programs. It's one of our many benefits from the microminiaturization forced by the extreme payload weight restrictions of the early rockets.

So the Large Scale Integrated circuit (LSI) was developed, wherein many thousands of discrete components like transistors, resistors, and other devices could be crammed on a tiny chip of silicon. This saved many pounds of weight in such on-board units as scientific instrumentation, telemetry radios, and computers. And the new LSI technology turned out to be especially well suited for use in computers. Computing devices that had once taken up most of a whole room could now be scrunched into a couple or three cubic feet of space. And, they were more efficient and cost a lot less to make, since the thumb-sized microprocessor LSI chip now replaced those thousands of not-so-cheap individual components. The microcomputer industry was born.

The microprocessor chip is actually the *whole* computer. Everything else inside the case merely supports the microprocessor. Mass producing this "chip" makes it cost even less. So, in the mid-seventies, companies like Motorola with their 6800 chip and Intel with their 8080 chip, put the microprocessor on the general market. Intel later became exceptionally successful with their 8088, 80236, and now the newest 80386 chip, one or the other of which is probably working in your computer right now.

Electronic hobbyists such as amateur radio operators were the first to take advantage of these computers-in-a chip. They begin designing and building the support circuitry necessary to turn the microprocessor chips into usable, full-fledged computers. Such companies as Southwest Technical Products and Altair quickly came on the market with kits of everything needed to put together your own computer. This is how I started, with a Southwest Tech MP6800 computer kit in 1976.

But computer kits were still limited to those of us who knew how to solder and were willing to do the many hours of work necessary in assembling and testing the machine—and finding our mistakes that kept it from working. Yet the interest shown by people in owning their very own computer was growing. The kits helped create the market for assembled units for only slightly more money. And the units were becoming more and more powerful.

Garage—sized operations like Apple sprang into being to meet the demands of this new market. The magic of having your very own personal computer had created the growth industry of the eighties, the microcomputer industry. Apple and Radio Shack and Commodore, along with many other small computer manufacturing operations, begin to reap the profits of the personal computer revolution, and to compete with one another in bringing out newer, less expensive, more powerful microcomputers. The computers got smaller and the little companies got bigger.

The big guys and gals, the IBMs and the DECs and the Data Generals, continued to ignore the microcomputer. Their public pronouncements were to the effect that the "home" computer was just a toy and of no utilitarian value. However, there was much speculation in the many magazines devoted to the microcomputer field that behind-the-scenes development was taking place to bring the major name, old-line computer companies into the personal computer market.

All this speculation was spurred on by the small business discovery of the microcomputer. Now it was possible for a hardware store or a doctor's office or a home remodeling service to computerize, just like their big corporate rivals. For just a few thousand dollars, these "mom and pop" operations could computerize. Beginning around 1980, tens of thousands of small businesses begin shopping for and purchasing microcomputer systems. The marketplace suddenly went into high gear.

Then the big boys dropped the other shoe. IBM announced their "Personal Computer," quickly followed by Digital Equipment Corporation, Burroughs, and a host of the other large computer manufacturers. But the little guys, like Apple, had grown up and were willing, even anxious, to compete.

Today, we're bombarded by computer-related advertising in virtually every publication we pick up. Television brings smiling computer salespersons into our very living rooms. All our friends, it seems, are buying computers or using them at the office, in school, or in their homes. The sheer immensity of the conflicting and confusing claims can drive the first-time shopper/user completely out of his/her mind. It's much like sticking your head out the door to see if there's any rain and being hit with a tidal wave.

While this book is about one particular package, there will be some general tips in it, as well as how to make some sense out of this plethora of information. After all, that's what artificial intelligence and Turbo Prolog is really all about—the management and use of information.

MOVING LOGICALLY ALONG

This chapter has been concerned with the *quest* for artificial intelligence. A lot of historical material has just been imparted; if I did my job well, it was interesting. We have discussed all this for a reason, to better help you understand and appreciate the importance and impact of artificial intelligence on Mankind in general and us—you and I—in particular.

The wonder of what has been done is fantastic. But what is to come, and that which you can do *right now* with AI programming languages such as Turbo Prolog, is even more wondrous. Let's move along into more practical information—the background on artificial intelligence and logic programming.

Chapter 2

Defining Prolog

TURBO PROLOG IS A TRUE JOY: A POWERFUL PROGRAMMING LANguage that's as easy for the computer novice to use as it is for the professional.

Before we look at Turbo Prolog in detail, let's install your program so you can follow examples on your computer as we discuss them. Doing examples as you read about them will help you understand and remember the concepts we are discussing.

INSTALLATION

The recommended basic hardware requirements to use Turbo Prolog are an IBM PC, XT, AT, or compatible computer with a minimum of 384K of RAM; an IBM Color Graphics Adapter or Enhanced Graphics Adapter (EGA) card, or equivalent; and PC- (or MS-) DOS 2.0 or newer versions. You can use Turbo Prolog without a graphics adapter but, of course, cannot use graphics in that case. Alas, the Hercules Monochrome card is not currently supported.

The two disks that come in the Turbo Prolog package are not copy protected. They may or may not be write-protected, so be careful!

- Two-Floppy Disk Systems: First make backup copies of the Turbo Prolog disks. Put the Turbo Prolog Program Disk in Drive A and one of your blank *system* disks in Drive B, type the command **copy A:*.***

B: and hit Enter to start it. This will take a short amount of time, and you will see a list of file names scroll onto your screen. You have instructed the computer to copy all files on Drive A to Drive B.

Do exactly the same operation for the Turbo Prolog Library Disk; this should be copied on one of your regular formatted disks, leaving one spare in case of emergencies. Label your new disks.

Here's the easy, faster way to back up disks. On the same utility disk as FORMAT is another program called DISKCOPY.COM. To use it, place a blank, unformatted disk in Drive B. Type **DISKCOPY A: B:** and press the Enter key. The computer will tell you to "place SOURCE DISK in A: and TARGET DISK in B:". *Take out* your system disk and replace it with the disk to be duplicated. Hit Enter again.

The beauty of this method is that the new disk is formatted as it copies, thus avoiding the time-consuming step of formatting detailed above. You can use DISKCOPY to make regular backups of your data disks.

- Hard Disk Systems: For you fixed-disk users, we must add a couple of operations.

Make sure your screen displays the C> prompt. Now place the Turbo Prolog Program Disk in Drive A and type this command:

DISKCOPY A: A:.

This is the easiest way to copy disks on a single-floppy system. Follow the instructions on the screen, changing between the Turbo Prolog program disk (SOURCE) and your blank disk (TARGET) as it instructs you. Make copies of the other disk in this same manner.

Installation: Put the Program Disk into Drive A and make sure your screen displays the C> prompt and is at the root directory. Confirm this by typing **cd** and hitting the Enter key. Then punch in the command **md \\prolog** and hit the Enter key. Next, enter **COPY A:*.*** and press Enter.

This creates a subdirectory on your fixed disk named PROLOG and copies all Turbo Prolog files from the Program Disk into the new directory.

The next step is to copy the Library Disk onto the hard disk. Remove the Program Disk from Drive A, insert the Library Disk, and type the command **COPY A:*.***. The files on this disk are now also copied into the new subdirectory. The computer will tell you when it is finished.

That done, remove the Library Disk from Drive A. Your backups are complete.

- The Print Screen (PrtSc) Key: Turbo Prolog can drive (with a little help) most dot-matrix printers beautifully, giving you a permanent hard copy of all the visual representations generated by the powerful graphics predicates in Turbo Prolog.

Other printers, such as thermal and the new wizard laser printers, also can be used with Turbo Prolog. If your printer is typewriter quality, however, like a daisy wheel or type-thimble device, you cannot do a screen print of graphs.

Assuming that you have printer capacity, a minor installation step is needed to convert the PrtSc key to a usable state. For two-floppy users, a program called GRAPHICS.COM should be on the DOS disk. Hard disk owners will find this same program in their root or DOS directories. This short utility must be installed to activate the PrtSc key, done simply by invoking it by typing **GRAPHICS**.

Folks with two drives who plan on using the Turbo Prolog Program Disk to bring up the computer from a power-off condition will now want to copy GRAPHICS.COM to that disk. To do so, place your DOS disk in A: and your working copy of the Turbo Prolog System Disk in B: type **COPY A:GRAPHICS.COM B:**. Hard disk users usually don't have to worry with this; GRAPHICS.COM should be available for use as it is. However, if the program is not in your root directory, put your DOS disk in Drive A and use the command **COPY A:GRAPHICS.COM C:**. If you plan to give the GRAPHICS command only after you change to the directory named PROLOG, you need to copy it to there or enter a path command so that it could be found from the PROLOG directory when called for. If it's already in your root directory, go to the PROLOG directory by using **CD\PROLOG** and issue the command **COPY C:GRAPHICS.COM**.

One thing to be aware of is that the graphics program on your DOS disk is designed to work with IBM, Epson, or other compatible dot-matrix printers having graphics capability, and with the IBM color graphics card. It will not work with other printers or some graphics cards. Usually other graphics adapters supply their own driver program, which you must load by name.

- Other Installation Tasks: There are some other things you might encounter in installation. One of the most likely is configuring for a serial printer instead of the IBM and compatibles' parallel interface. Consult the information on the MODE command in your DOS manual. This will give you the format you need to construct a command to be added to your AUTOEXEC file, if you use one, which will automatically switch to the correct configuration to let Turbo Prolog communicate with a serial printer.

Another common thing is adding a *mouse*, a hand-held input device that will cause the cursor on your computer screen to move accordingly. If you want to use Turbo Prolog with one of these devices, there is usually a mouse "driver" program that must be loaded first. This is something else to add to an AUTOEXEC file. The precise procedure needed to activate your mouse will be included in the documentation that came with it.

Now that you've installed Turbo Prolog, you can boot it up:

- Two-Drive Systems—Put your Turbo Prolog working disk into Drive A and type **PROLOG**, followed by a press of the Return key to inform your computer that the proper command is entered and it may now act on it.
- Hard Disk Systems—Change to the subdirectory containing the Prolog programs (typing **CD \ PROLOG** to access it). Then enter **PROLOG** to invoke the programming environment.

After a few seconds of disk drive whirring, Turbo Prolog's initial copyright screen appears; at the bottom you will notice the message "Press the SPACE bar." Doing so will cause the program to put you into the programming environment.

First examine the copyright screen. There are two smaller boxes, both inside the larger one that outlines the whole screen. The top box is labeled "Turbo Prolog" and has Borland's copyright information, their corporate name, and the version number of this particular Turbo Prolog package.

The current version number of Turbo Prolog is 1.1. If your version number of Turbo Prolog is not 1.1, then you need to contact the supplier from whom you purchased Turbo Prolog for your free upgrade.

The second small box on the screen is labeled "Configuration," in which one file and four directories are indicated. The file in the configuration box your programming environment is initialized to normally is WORK.PRO. This means that any new program you start will be called "WORK" until you rename it. The .PRO extension must be present for Turbo Prolog to recognize it as a Prolog program file. The four directories come initialized to Drive A. This is fine for the moment if you are using a two-drive system. Those who have hard disks need to make some easy changes. Simply change all default settings, A:\, to C:\ *plus* the name of the subdirectory in which your programs will reside.

WHAT IS PROLOG?

Prolog (*PRO*gramming in *LOG*ic) is a *declarative* language, allowing representation of data in *symbolic* logic. In such a language, programs use deductive reasoning to solve problems. Given a set of facts and the rules determining interrelationships, Prolog answers questions without requiring you to worry about *how* it is done. BASIC, Pascal, C, Fortran, and all the other traditional computer languages are *procedural*—the programmer must supply an involved set of step-by-step instructions to accomplish the end result.

Prolog is much simpler; only a description of the problem (the *goal*) and the ground rules for solving it are required. Prolog then automatically determines the best method to implement the goal. Turbo Prolog programs typically can be as much as 10 times shorter than a BASIC or Pascal program that does the same thing.

Prolog is an Artificial Intelligence (AI) language.

WHAT IS ARTIFICIAL INTELLIGENCE?

Computers using AI operate in a "relational" mode, similar to the way our own brains do, rather than in the discrete memory address format into which they are currently frozen. The *relational* mode will be a marked improvement. It works, in very simple analogy, like this: If I say the word *red,* you might think of various objects or conditions that fall in a class loosely associated with "red-ness": tomatoes, perhaps, or hearts, faces of embarrassed people, the Washington Redskins, apples.

Having the general class, you can easily and quickly proceed from there within the context of the other search parameters given. If we are indeed thinking about apples as a fruit, then the words "Granny Smith" will mean one of that class, all of which grow on trees. This relational or associative capacity will make computers operate much faster and programs will be a lot smaller and more powerful.

Programs based on the concepts of artificial intelligence can be and are being written, programs that behave intelligently, flexibly, and exhibit human-like understanding. This concept is called "natural language." Simply put, instead of convoluted commands to achieve an end, the user just types in normal English. Programs also can be "expert," knowing more than we, the users, about a given specialty.

Not that this is some technique springing full-grown from the brow of the world's greatest software engineer (which is what some programmers like to be called these days). No, artificial intelligence theory has been around for quite some time. A classic AI demo is a little game called "Animals." This early simulation was written in 1973 by Nathan Teichholtz of Digital Equipment Corporation; a Turbo Prolog version is included in Borland's package (Fig. 2-1). Now AI is no longer just a toy, it's useful, as will be shown in this book with Turbo Prolog.

"Once you've worked with software that reflects your own thinking," says Mike Edelhart, a former editor of *PC Magazine,* "it's hard to be satisfied with anything less." Mr. Edelhart, in this statement, is describing one of the practical AI programming development systems now available for the widely based IBM PC and PC-compatible computers. Called Expert Ease, the software is an AI *system generator* that is, in the words of its maker, Human Edge Systems, "just waiting to be-

```
┌──────────────────────────────────────────────────────────────────────────┐
|      Run       Compile      Edit       Options       Files      Setup      Quit    |
└──────────────────────────────────────────────────────────────────────────┘
┌──────────────────────────────── Editor ──────┌────────── Dialog ──────────┐
| Line 1       Col 1      Indent   Insert  EXAMPL51.P|yes                       |
|/* Program 51 */                                  |has it long_neck           |
|/*                                                |no                        |
| For a more complete sample expert system, see    |has it black_stripes      |
| the program GENI.PRO on the LIBRARY DISK         |yes                       |
|*/                                                |                          |
|database                                          |Your animal may be a(n) zebr|
|     xpositive(symbol,symbol)                     |a                         |
|     xnegative(symbol,symbol)                     |                          |
|                                                  |                          |
|predicates                                        |                          |
|     run                                          |Please press the space bar t|
|     animal_is(symbol)                            |o Exit                    |
|     it_is(symbol)                                └──────────────────────────┘
┌──────────────────── Message ─────────────────┐                              |
|negative                                      |                              |
|clear_facts                                   |                              |
|remember                                      |                              |
|ask                                           |                              |
└──────────────────────────────────────────────┘──────────────────────────────┘
Use first letter of option  or  select with  ->  or  <-
```

Fig. 2-1. "Animals" is one of the classic artificial intelligence demo programs. A simple Turbo Prolog version is included with your package as EXAMPLE51.PRO.

come as smart and savvy as you are." Essentially, the software allows an expert, in whatever field, to enter problem solving information by example.

Expert Ease learns from this, automatically constructing appropriate decision trees. The end result is that programs generated by this method allow non-experts to make a decision, solve a problem, or otherwise have the benefit of expert advice as if the expert were actually there. The created program becomes the expert. We'll look at how to create programs of this type using Turbo Prolog.

PROLOG VS. BASIC

Let's look at a quick example of how a Prolog program looks and acts compared with an equivalent BASIC program. A program based on the statements "John likes Mary" and "Bill likes the ladies that John likes" can be written in either Prolog or a conventional language. However, making the program answer the question, "Whom does Bill like?" can be very convoluted in the older languages. As complexity increases, the older programming languages are quickly outstripped by Prolog's efficiency and power.

The older languages are closely tied to computer hardware. In these *imperative* or *procedural* languages, every step the computer takes to determine the answer to a question must be spelled out in exact, nit-picking detail.

To answer the question made from combining the two statements above, "*Who does Bill like if Bill likes who John likes?*" can be done in BASIC (Fig. 2-2). The procedure is moderately simple: state the data, read it into a variable array, then set up a loop to do a comparison that determines who John likes—which of course meets the criteria set up by the rules and answers the question.

With the MID$ and LEN statements, however, you can see that the program is quickly approaching unwieldy complexity. Add several more rules, plug in more data, and soon there will be several hundred command lines. There is also an underlying *flaw* to answering these types of questions in BASIC (or Pascal or C).

The BASIC program cannot answer any *other* question on the relationships stated in the data. Ask it who Rhett or Marvin likes and all you'll get back is an "Insufficient or incorrect data" statement.

The equivalent Turbo Prolog program (Fig. 2-3) is shorter than the BASIC version, but considerably more powerful. Note that there are no commands for procedures as in the BASIC program. We don't have to devise instructions telling Prolog to read in the variables and compare

```
10 REM :::::: a BASIC program to find out who Bill likes ::::::
20 REM :::::: written by Ralph Roberts :::::::::::::::::::::::
30 REM
40 DATA CHARLIE LIKES SUE ELLEN
50 DATA FARLEY LIKES WANDA
60 DATA RHETT LIKES MISS SCARLETT
70 DATA MARVIN LIKES PEARL
80 DATA JOHN LIKES MARY
90 FOR X=1 TO 5:READ A$(X):NEXT X
100 INPUT "Name ";B$
110 IF B$="BILL" THEN LET B$="JOHN" ELSE GOTO 210
120 PRINT
130 FOR X=1 TO 5
140 C$=""
150 FOR Y=1 TO LEN(A$(X))
160 IF MID$(A$(X),Y,1)=" " THEN 190
170 C$=C$+MID$(A$(X),Y,1)
180 NEXT Y
190 IF C$=B$ THEN 220
200 NEXT X
210 PRINT "Insufficient  or incorrect data.":PRINT:GOTO 230
220 PRINT "BILL";MID$(A$(X),Y,LEN(A$(X))-Y+1)
230 END
```

Fig. 2-2. A sample BASIC program showing the convoluted means of handling logic in procedural languages.

```
domains
    person, lady = symbol

predicates
    likes(person,lady)

clauses
    likes(charlie,sue_ellen).
    likes(farley,wanda).
    likes(rhett,miss_scarlett).
    likes(marvin,pearl).
    likes(john,mary).
    likes(bill,X) if likes(john,X).
```

Fig. 2-3. A shorter and more powerful way to do logic programming is in a declarative language such as Turbo Prolog.

them, as in the BASIC program. Turbo Prolog knows how to do all that on its own. All we have to do is declare the rules and relationships.

Three categories are all that is needed to find out who Bill likes. The first is *domains*, which specifies the types of values that objects may take in relation to each other. Here lady is declared to be a symbol.

This is followed by the *predicate* declaration. Every Turbo Prolog fact or rule belongs to some predicate which specifies the name of the relation involved and the types of objects involved in this relation. In our example we are declaring that *a person likes a certain lady.* In Prolog this is entered as likes(person,lady).

The third major area of declaration in our example are the *clauses*—the rules for a particular predicate. The clauses define who likes whom. The first is likes(charlie,sue_ellen). Charlie is a specific person and Sue Ellen is the lady he specifically likes. The last clause entered is likes(bill,X) if likes (john,X). This is the rule stating that Bill likes ladies that John likes.

Once this information is entered, that's all there is to the program. Turbo Prolog does the rest.

Those of you who are sitting in front of your computers and following along with this book might want to create this program and try it. I strongly recommend the hands-on method of learning.

When the program is run, a *dialog window* (letting you talk to Prolog) is opened. You can then ask a number of questions by typing in the correct syntax. Prolog requests the goal. To find out who Bill likes, we can ask in two ways. The first, likes(bill,Who), will return Who = mary because the program recognizes the rules that John likes Mary and Bill likes who John likes. Thus it meets the goal we specified.

Alternatively, you could input likes(bill,mary). Here we're really asking, "Does Bill like Mary?" Prolog applies the rules we declared to it,

```
    Run        Compile        Edit        Options        Files        Setup        Quit

-------------------- Editor --------------------  ---------------- Dialog ----------------
 Line 1      Col 1      Indent   Insert   EXAMPL01.
/* Program 1 */
/*
   Enter the goal on page 18 of the manual.
   Some valuable notes are at the bottom
   of this program.        ------------------ Help ---------------------------------------
*/
                           F U N C T I O N   K E Y S        SPECIAL COMBINATION
domains
    person, activity = s     F1              F2              Ctrl   <-    Move t
                             Pop-Up          Goto to Line
predicates                   Help                            Ctrl   ->    Move t
    likes(person,activit
                             F3              F4              Ctrl   PgUp  Goto t
clauses                      Search          Replace
    likes(ellen,tennis).     Srch Again      R. Again        Ctrl   PgDn  Goto t
    likes(john,football)
    likes(tom,baseball).     F5              F6              Ctrl   Home  Goto s
    likes(eric,swimming)

F2:Goto line     F3:Search     S-F10:Resize window     F10:End
```

Fig. 2-4. The programming environment is the main screen of Turbo Prolog. It includes features such as the "help" pop-up window shown here.

```
    Run        Compile        Edit        Options        Files        Setup        Quit

-------------------- Editor ------------------- Load                   g -------------
 Line 1      Col 1      Indent   Inser
                                      Directory: B:\EXAMPLES
                                      File mask: *.PRO
                 ---------------- Directory: B:\EXAMPLES\*.PRO ----------------
                  EXAMPL01.PRO   EXAMPL02.PRO   EXAMPL03.PRO   EXAMPL04.PRO
                  EXAMPL05.PRO   EXAMPL06.PRO   EXAMPL07.PRO   EXAMPL08.PRO
                  EXAMPL09.PRO   EXAMPL10.PRO   EXAMPL11.PRO   EXAMPL12.PRO
                  EXAMPL13.PRO   EXAMPL14.PRO   EXAMPL15.PRO   EXAMPL16.PRO
                  EXAMPL17.PRO   EXAMPL18.PRO   EXAMPL19.PRO   EXAMPL20.PRO
                  EXAMPL21.PRO   EXAMPL22.PRO   EXAMPL23.PRO   EXAMPL24.PRO
                  EXAMPL25.PRO   EXAMPL26.PRO   EXAMPL27.PRO   EXAMPL28.PRO
                  EXAMPL29.PRO   EXAMPL30.PRO   EXAMPL31.PRO   EXAMPL32.PRO
                  EXAMPL33.PRO   EXAMPL34.PRO   EXAMPL35.PRO   EXAMPL36.PRO

                                                   ------------- Trace -------------

PgUp,PgDn and <-,->:Move cursor   S-F10:Resize window   Esc:End
```

Fig. 2-5. File management also can be done via pop-up windows.

```
   Run       Compile      Edit       Options       Files       Setup       Quit

--------------------------------- Editor ---------------------------------------
  Line 1      Col 1       Indent   Insert   SANAL.PRO
/* SENTENCE ANALYSIS */
/*
  This sample shows how sentence analysis
  can be done in TURBO-PROLOG.

  As an example, the following sentence
  can be recognized:
"every man that lives loves a woman"
*/

DATABASE    /* words which can be recognized */
  noun( STRING )
  det( STRING )
  rel( STRING )
  verb( STRING )

include "menu.pro"

Use first letter of option  or  select with  ->  or  <-
```

Fig. 2-6. Turbo Prolog is especially well suited to natural language recognition, one of the underlying concepts of artificial intelligence.

```
   Run       Compile      Edit       Options       Files       Setup       Quit

--------------------------------- Editor ---------------------------------------
  Line 1      Col 1       Indent   Insert   ANS30.PRO
/* Answer to exercise on Page 30 */
/*
  This is an exercise in domain declarations and
  predicate declarations, not a test of your
  ability to solve  murder mysteries. We have
  made some modifications to the program in the
  book to placate those who must have a killer.

  Enter the goal
      killer(X).

  Bert is guilty because he has a motive and is
  smeared in the same stuff as the victim. (Use
  trace to follow the resolution of the crime)
*/

domains
    name, sex, occupation, object, vice, substance = symbol

Use first letter of option  or  select with  ->  or  <-
```

Fig. 2-7. Turbo Prolog also is well suited to expert systems, the other major thrust of artificial intelligence.

```
    Run      Compile      Edit      Options      Files      Setup      Quit

-------------------------------- Editor --------------------------------
  Line 1      Col 1      Indent  Insert  EXAMPL64.PRO
/*
  This is a sample Turbo Prolog program
  that calls C Language routines. See
  EXAMPL65.C for more information.  Read
  the READ64.ME file on this disk for
  more information.
*/

global domains
  ilist = integer*
  ifunc = f(integer)

global predicates
  clist(ilist, ifunc) - (i,o) (o,i) language c

goal
  clearwindow,
  clist(°3§,X),

Use first letter of option  or  select with  ->  or  <-
```

Fig. 2-8. Interfacing routines for calling existing programs in other languages also are provided in Turbo Prolog.

```
    Run      Compile      Edit      Options      Files      Setup      Quit

-------------------------------- Editor --------------------------------
  Line 1      Col 1      Indent  Insert  EXAMPL56.PRO
/* Program 56 */
/*
  This program attempts to divide words into
  syllables.
*/

domains
    letter = char
    word = letter*

predicates
    divide(word,word,word,word)
    vocal(letter)
    consonant(letter)
    string_word(string,word)
    append(word,word,word)

goal

Use first letter of option  or  select with  ->  or  <-
```

Fig. 2-9. One of Turbo Prolog's main strengths is its ability to handle words, such as in this sample hyphenation program.

sees that John likes Mary and Bill likes who John likes, and thus the program responds with the word **True**.

Here's a third way we could ask: **likes(Who,mary)** (or, "Who likes Mary?"). Again the rules are applied and *two* answers are found: **Who = john** and **Who = bill** because, according to our declared rules, both John and Bill like her.

Prolog obviously is much more powerful than BASIC, so rather than just find the single relationship that our sample BASIC program did, Prolog allows much more flexibility. By inquiring **likes(Who,Lady)**, we can get a complete list of all relationships, such as **Who = charlie**, **Lady = sue_ellen** and so on. There are a total of six solutions, including two for Mary. To do all this in BASIC would take a great deal more programming time.

This example is only one of the many ways in which Turbo Prolog, a fifth-generation language, transcends older methods of programming. Which does not mean that it totally replaces them; some "number crunching" applications are better done in a procedural-type language. Different tools are appropriate for different jobs.

Figures 2-4 through 2-9 illustrate some of the features of the Turbo Prolog programming environment.

Chapter 3

A Closer Look At The Differences

SINCE 1972 A NUMBER OF PROLOG IMPLEMENTATIONS HAVE APpeared. Each varies widely in syntax. Prolog, like BASIC, is far from standard and, also like BASIC, a variety of dialects exist. Borland's Turbo Prolog is spoken with a Pascal accent rather the lilting tones of pure Prolog. As with anything, this has advantages and disadvantages.

THE AI CONNECTION

In the field of pure research, AI techniques currently are concerned with two major areas that computer technology has not handled well in the past. These are natural language interfacing and visually making sense of the world. *Natural language recognition* is the ability of a program to accept and successfully understand common, everyday sentences in your language. No special syntax is required for command structures. Borland's Turbo Prolog is quite adept at natural language interfacing. It can *parse*, i.e., take a regular sentence like, "What cities are in North Carolina?" and respond with "Asheville, Charlotte, Winston-Salem, Greensboro, and Raleigh." Or it can give the same answer to such variations on the question as "List cities in North Carolina" or "North Carolina cities?" or "cities, NC?"

The second major area of AI research, *visual interpretation* by the computer of what is going on around it, still lies largely in the future. It is not something that Turbo Prolog running on a PC, AT, or equivalent computer is going to have enough power to do well. Still, the natural language capacity alone will open up a whole new world for you!

Error Tolerance

One of the most useful things that natural language ability translates into is *error tolerance.* We've noted that in procedural languages each and every step the computer takes must be spelled out in exact sequence and syntax. A tiny item like a missing comma in a data retrieval instruction can cause much irritation. A good programmer will do such things as make his or her program accept upper- or lowercase entries, and put proper error trapping in place. Good software, at least in obvious cases of command misstatements by the user, loops back to give him or her another shot at it.

Human fallibility, however, is not restricted to the end user. Programmers make mistakes. Errors in the coding of commands that determine syntax can be subtle and very frustrating. Then there also is the chance that whoever gathered and entered the data made a mistake. Even on personal computers, a database can consist of many thousand entries. A spelling error in the database would make that part of the database irritatingly inaccessible.

The term "fuzzy" is important. Software needs to be able to accept information that is merely *close* in spelling, capitalization, and *meaning.*

"Expert" Programs

There is much more to "non-exactness" than being able to handle the unexpected. The data we use in our daily lives is seldom clear and certain. We need the ability to ask for and get expert answers to questions in specific fields:

This man has a fever and is perspiring heavily. What is wrong with him?
There are traces of blue clay on this property. What minerals should I look for?
We are going to begin manufacturing the device described by the specifications in file GIZMO. Please give me a list allocating our various machine tools, and also one of the parts we should order.
Do we have enough ink to print this month's issue?
The victim was strangled with rope made of India hemp. Have there been any similar crimes in the last year?

Or my favorite, for which I'm writing an "expert" program:

I need a Turbo Prolog program to manage a database consisting of the structure in file ARTICLES.SLD. What predicates must I include?

Each of the above questions are phrased in plain English and are questions we would ask respectively of such experts as a doctor, a geologist, an industrial engineer, a print shop foreman, a criminal investigator, and a proficient Turbo Prolog programmer. The questions are phrased in the way we would ask a human expert, and our query would be understood.

Given the proper program, a human expert can answer a series of questions, the software can store them, and when you ask the program questions it will answer as if the expert were there. The "fuzzy" part is accomplished by *weighting* the expert's opinions. He or she may be 60 percent certain that if certain facts are present, a specific result may have a better than average chance of occurring. By asking and obtaining answers to a series of related questions, you can obtain an even greater percentage of certainty. This is what an expert system does.

Constructing a viable expert system takes more than just programming wizardry. Any expert, human or cybernetic, is only as good as the sum of his or her knowledge. The system consists of *rules*. A doctor examining a patient applies the rules, usually without even thinking about them: "A temperature of 101? *Hmmm*. This man is sick, so I should continue. He is coughing. Using my stethoscope, I find that his chest is congested. Pneumonia? Just a chest cold? Flu symptoms?" The doctor then involves other rules to narrow the possibilities down even more until he is reasonably certain of the problem. "You have the flu, Mr. Jones. The nurse will give you a shot. Then I want you to go home and get lots of rest."

An expert medical program can do all of the above. Much more complicated diagnoses are being handled now by medical expert systems. The equivalent is true in many other fields as well. Expert systems are important applications of AI and Prolog programming.

LOGIC PROGRAMMING

Logic programming depends heavily on the concept of *backward reasoning* or *backtracking*. Backtracking may be boiled down to the statement that "A is true if B and C exist." Using this technique, declared rules take the place of the exact, detailed procedural invocations used in older languages. But through backtracking, Prolog also may be used as a purely procedural language.

A bit of clarification is necessary. "Procedural" as applied to older languages and to Prolog has a slightly different meaning—a shading, not an outright difference. In BASIC, C, Pascal, and the others, we must specify not only how the problems are to be resolved, but also the way in which the computer does it, step by laborious step. A procedural implementation in Prolog, however, simply refers to detailing the order in which a problem is to be solved, not the machine instructions.

Unlike software written in other languages, which are essentially collections of functions, a Prolog program is a sequence of relations and rules about a subject (Fig. 3-1). These make up a *database* of facts that can be queried or added to (Fig. 3-2).

Here are three examples of rules:

```
likes(ralph,prolog)
likes(reader,prolog) if explains(ralph,prolog)
explains(ralph,prolog)
```

Expressed in plain English, these simply state that Ralph likes Prolog, the reader will like Prolog if Ralph explains it, and that Ralph explains Prolog.

In our example, we need to specify no procedures to obtain results; we merely query the "database" of known facts. These facts, called *clauses*, are one of the four major parts of a Turbo Prolog program (the other three being domains, predicates, and the goal or goals).

When this little program is invoked under Turbo Prolog, a dialog window appears and the word "Goal:" appears. We may now ask various questions. Entering likes(Who,prolog) and hitting the Return key gives us two answers, Who = ralph and Who = reader. (Variables start with capital letters, and we are free to choose descriptive words for them, such as "Who" in this case.)

Here's how Prolog achieved these results logically. (Remember, please, we specified no procedure but simply declared the three clauses or rules.) The last clause, explains(ralph,prolog) is examined and found to be a statement of fact, i.e., no conditions are attached. It tells the program that I explain Prolog, but it does not satisfy the goal, so backtracking continues to the next clause, which is:

```
likes(reader,prolog) if explains(ralph,prolog)
```

```
domains
        prolog, person = symbol

predicates

        likes(person,prolog)
        explains(person,prolog)

clauses

        likes(ralph,prolog).
        likes(reader,prolog) if explains(ralph,prolog).
        explains(ralph,prolog).
```

Fig. 3-1. Turbo Prolog programs are simple structures in normal text using declarative logic.

```
|    Run      Compile      Edit      Options      Files      Setup      Quit    |

------------------------------- Editor ----------------------------------------
|  Line 1      Col 1      Indent   Insert   ANS71.PRO
|/* Answer to exercise on Page 71 */
|
|domains
|     name, address_str, town = string
|     zip = integer
|     address = address(name, address_str, town, zip).
|
|predicates
|     printAddress(address)
|     start
|
|goal
|     start.
|
|clauses
|     printAddress(address(N,A,T,Z)):-
|          write(N),nl,
|          write(A),nl,

Use first letter of option  or  select with  ->  or  <-
```

Fig. 3-2. Handling database information is a snap with Turbo Prolog.

Here exists the standard conclusion-condition format. Prolog backtracks through it, first encountering the rule behind the "if," and finds that it already knows this fact. So the likes(reader,prolog) part is returned as true and the goal Who = reader obtains.

But wait! Prolog is not satisfied with just achieving one goal. It will now backtrack through the clauses to see if any others fit. The rule likes(ralph,prolog) is now found and the second answer, Who = ralph, is added. No other conclusions can be reached, so the program prints out its conclusions.

Note that we did not tell the program how to do it; we merely gave it some rules and asked a question. We may ask it other questions as well. Typing in explains(Who,What) returns Who = ralph and What = prolog. Instead of just the limited facts the program now knows, we could keep adding rules in the format explains(who,what) until the same general question asked above would give us hundreds or thousands of answers. In fact, we would have to be more specific, elaborating the logic, or be flooded with answers such as:

```
Who = pete_rose, What = baseball
Who = liberace, What = piano_playing
Who = dan_rather, What = evening_news
```

and so on.

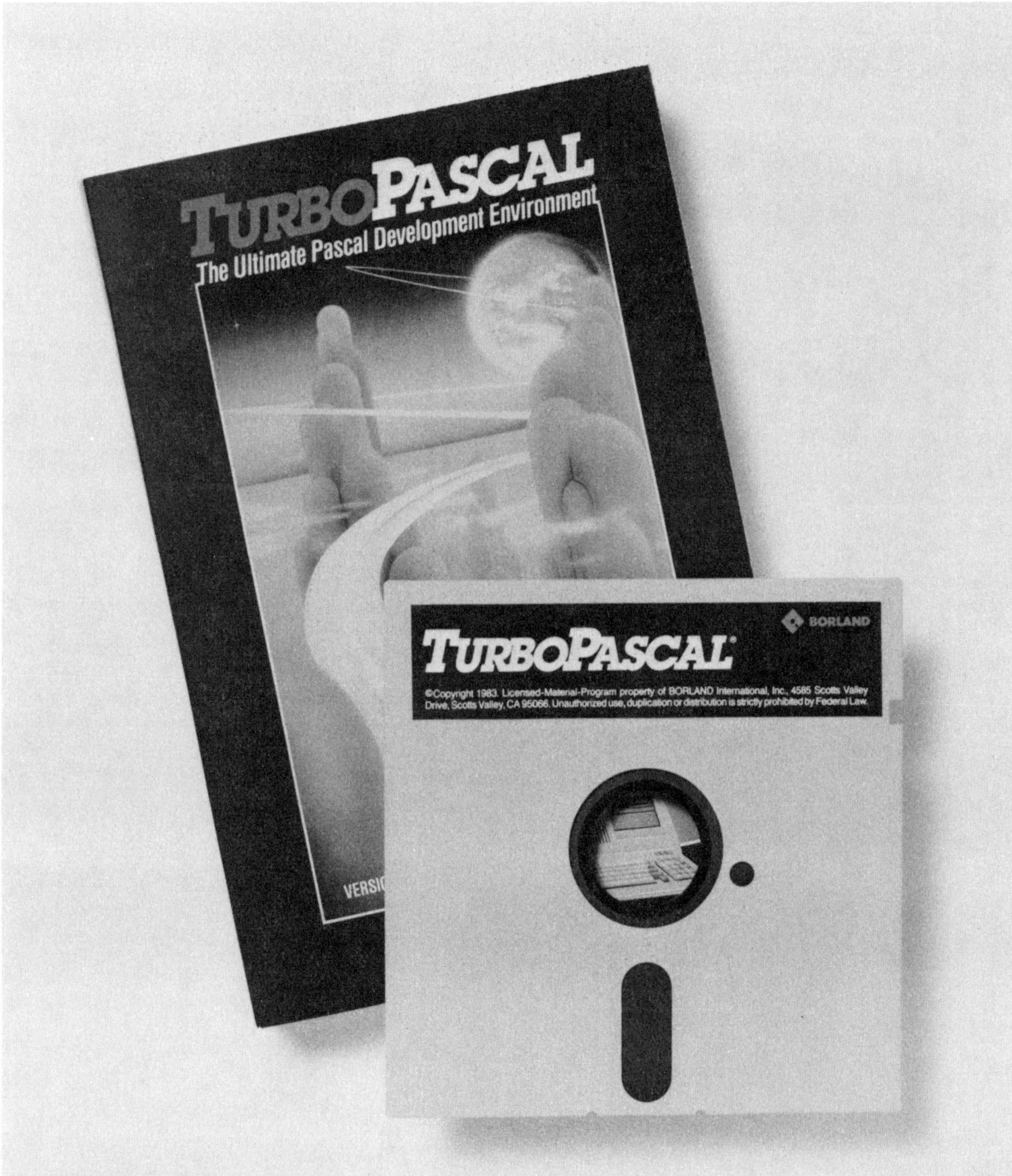

Fig. 3-3. Turbo Prolog shows a certain amount of the influence from Turbo Pascal, one of Borland's largest software successes.

Fig. 3-4. The Reflex database manager, another popular Borland product.

Fig. 3-5. Borland's Sidekick is a set of memory-resident utilities that can be of great use to programmers.

What we did above was to discover "facts." Just as easy is checking to see if a fact is true. The goal **explains(ralph,prolog)** will return the answer **true**. Thus we could have a goal that depends on finding certain subgoals true or false.

Essentially, then, backtracking works backward from the conclusion of a statement existing in the form "conclusion if conditions," reducing problems into subproblems that match the conditions given as it goes. *This* is the essence of how Turbo Prolog works!

Here's an example of using backtracking procedurally. Let's say you work for software company Borland. You want to write a program in Turbo Prolog to help sell the package as well as some of the company's other products—Turbo Pascal, another programming language; Reflex, a database manager and Sidekick, a set of memory-resident utilities (Figs. 3-3, 3-4, and 3-5). You have a database consisting of everybody in the world and their occupation. What logic should be used to generate a mailing of the proper information to the proper person?

The conclusion part of the statement is pretty obvious; "*x* can be sold to *y*." There are a number of conditions that must be applied, however. All inhabitants of the Amazon rain forest with the occupation of head hunter are not likely to be good prospects for Turbo Prolog. Thus, you want to specify that only certain job classifications are acceptable. Adding such a condition gives us "*x* can be sold to *y* if *y* has occupation *z*."

That's simple enough so far, but remember that we have several products. How does the program know which product to match to which occupation? Another condition is needed. You must specify which jobs could use which software packages. The final statement is now formulated and reads: "*x* can be sold to *y* if *y* has occupation *z* and *x* can be used for *z*."

Now! Controlled backtracking! The Turbo Prolog program begins with the last first. It checks the occupations, thus eliminating candlestick makers, bakers, and head hunters. In the parlance of Turbo Prolog, the tests for these are said to *fail*, which in itself causes backtracking through the list to try the next person's job description. The test succeeds only for the designated occupations—writer, salesperson, programmer. Once a match occurs, the proper product is chosen and the program backtracks to the next condition. It keeps trying until a person is found who is also a writer. Then the conclusion is reached. The person is a writer and can be sold Lightning. A literature packet is sent out.

Chapter 4

Turbo Prolog Features

BEFORE WE GET INTO ACTUAL PROGRAM OPERATION, LET'S TAKE a look at some of the features you get with Turbo Prolog, and explore some of the ways the Turbo version varies from other versions of Prolog.

VERSION 1.1

Version 1.1 of Turbo Prolog is Borland's most recent enhancement of their original Prolog software. Any owner of the earlier release will be given a free upgrade to Version 1.1.

Most important, Version 1.1 is a more powerful language that uses less working memory space. More predicates, necessary for natural language databases and expert systems, are included. The free upgrade delivers a three-fold increase in compilation speed. An internal linker, featuring single-step compiling into executable (EXE) files has been included.

The new compile option lets you compile and link all modules for a given project automatically. You can have configuration files for programs, which means that you can easily set up customized installations of windows and colors without having to change the program and compile it all over again.

The enhancement provides more than 100 examples, including step-by-step instructions for modifying and linking Assembler and C programs.

Several advanced programs include an expert system example, a sentence analyzer, and a symbolic differentiation program.

Here are installation instructions. The example programs on the Library and Sample Programs disk that comes with Version 1.1 has the programs in *subdirectories*. Put the Sample Programs disk into Drive A on your computer. From the A> prompt, type the command **DIR** (which lists the files on the disk). If you have a hard disk system, type A: to make the A> prompt appear before issuing the **DIR** command.

There are five listings. The first two, PROLOG.LIB and INIT.OBJ, are files included with Version 1.0. The last three—EXAMPLES, ANSWERS, and PROGRAMS—all have the indication **<DIR>** following them. These are subdirectories, and must be accessed in order to copy them to another disk or to use the programs they contain.

Again from the A> prompt, enter the command **CD\EXAMPLES** in either upper- or lowercase. This changes the directory to the subdirectory EXAMPLES. Type **DIR** now and 74 example files are listed; issuing **DIR/W** instead will put these in five columns on your screen so that you can see all of them at once. While this subdirectory is selected, you may copy the files to your back up disk or to the Prolog subdirectory on a hard disk. To return to the main directory, type **CD**.

ADDITIONAL PREDICATES

A surprising omission in the first version of Turbo Prolog was the inability to have programs read and act on a named file from DOS, such as a utility to view the contents of a file. The predicate **comline**, included in Version 1.1, repairs this omission. It is now possible for a compiled Prolog program to read the command line parameters when a program is first called.

A new unbuffered window predicate, **GotoWindow**, has been added; it allows very fast shifts between two windows which do not overlap. It also lets you keep one window on the screen while shifting to a window behind it.

The **scroll** predicate indicates the number of lines to scroll in the active window:

```
scroll(NoOfRows,NoOfCols)
```

where **NoOfRows** indicates the number of lines to be scrolled up or down. A positive number scrolls up, a negative number scrolls down. **NoOfCols** indicates the number of columns to be scrolled left or right. A positive number scrolls left and a negative number scrolls right.

The new **filemode** predicate is for accessing binary files, which can be accomplished with the following command format:

```
filemode (SymbolicFileName, FileMode)
```

where **FileMode** specifies text mode (0) or binary mode (1).

Keypressed is also a new predefined predicate. This one makes it possible to test for a key pressed without reading the keystroke. The predicate **keypressed** succeeds if any key has been pressed, otherwise it fails.

In the graphics mode, the predicates **right** and **left** were not supported with an **o-flowpattern** in Version 1.0 of Turbo Prolog. A new predicate, called **penpos** (pen position), is in Version 1.1. This predicate can be used in two ways. If all parameters are bound prior to calling **penpos**, the predicate sets the position and direction of the turtle. If all parameters are free, they will be bound with the turtle's current position.

Included also with the Turbo Prolog 1.1 package is a small booklet that supplements the *Owner's Handbook*. The bulk of it is corrections to the handbook.

THE FLAVOR OF PASCAL

Turbo Prolog, to the dismay of some AI programmers, appears to have made some compromises so as to be more familiar to those proficient in Pascal. The primary compromise is *domain typing* of variables and the *declaration* of predicates (a predicate is a statement of relationship, e.g., **person(name)** telling Prolog that each name belongs to a person). This typing means a variable is declared at the beginning of the program as being a string of characters, a single character, a real or integer number, a file, or a "symbol."

The major difference is that other implementations of Prolog do not require predicate and variable "typing." This means that any logical operation or predicate that can build new forms of terms during actual operation of the program, rather than at compile time, is not found in Turbo Prolog.

In fact, the one real disappointment I have with this package is the restraint that data typing forces upon you. Most artificial intelligence languages, applications, and expert systems rely to great extent on databases to hold and receive queries on their accumulated information. The "standard" Prologs which adhere to the Clocksin and Mellish* guidelines are characterized by being able to add and use a wide range of user-supplied clauses, rules, and facts while running. These "standard" Prologs are considerably more flexible than Turbo Prolog in this respect.

While this restriction on flexibility does limit Borland's implementation somewhat or, requires extra hacking to achieve certain results that are standard predicates in other Prologs, there is an up side, too. Turbo

---

*W.F Clocksin and C.S. Mellish, *Programming in Prolog* (New York: Springer-Verlag, 1984).

Prolog does many things *better* than the "standards." And domains typing *does* make it easier for a Pascal programmer to learn.

Like Pascal, Turbo Prolog is a strongly "typed" language. These types are called *domains*. Domains specify the types of values that objects may take in relation to one another. The types of domains built into Turbo Prolog include *integer* (whole numbers from −32768 to 32767), *real* (real numbers such as 12.563 and 234.8), *character* (like "a" or "T"), *strings* ("this is a string of characters"), *file*, and *symbol*.

The last two domains need a bit more explanation. Turbo Prolog has several predefined *files* which you do not have to—and should not—declare in programs (rather like **input** and **output** in standard Pascal). These are *printer, keyboard, screen*, and the *COM1* port. Note that *printer* refers to the parallel printer port on the IBM PC and compatibles, while *COM1* is the serial port. What you do have to declare at the beginning of a program are the symbolic names for the actual data files that you intend to access during the course of its run. There can be only one file declaration line, so all of them must go on that line, separated by a semicolon, as in:

```
files = hisfile; herfile; itsfile
```

The last domain is the *symbol*, which is usually called an "atom" in Clocksin and Mellish implementations. It is the best domain to use for representing people and things. A symbol is just a name, and always begins with a lowercase letter.

As in Pascal, and distinct from other Prologs, Turbo Prolog programs have several discrete sections. The first is the *domains section* (indicated simply by the word **domains** flush against the left margin). Here variable typing is declared, such as:

```
expenses = real
vendor = symbol
product = string
```

and so forth.

The second section contains the predicates and begins where the word **predicates** is found again flush against the left margin. Predicates define the relationships. An example would be **person(name)**, where **name** is a symbol domain (Fig. 4-1). This predicate describes series of clauses or rules found in the clauses section.

Once more, a section's beginning is defined by its name flush against the left hand margin, in this case **clauses**. Clauses are the rules and relationships defined by the predicates and made up of various domains. For example, the simple predicate **person(name)** could define the clauses **per-**

```
domains
        name = symbol
predicates
        person(name)
clauses
        person(monica).
        person(heather).
        person(kimberly).
        person(susie).
```

Fig. 4-1. A simple program in Turbo Prolog.

```
domains
        name = symbol
predicates
        person(name)
goal
        person(Who),
        write(Who).

clauses
        person(monica).
        person(heather).
        person(kimberly).
        person(susie).
```

Fig. 4-2. Adding a goal section to a Turbo Prolog program allows external input.

son(monica), person(heather), person(kimberly), person(susie).

Unlike many Prologs, you may also specify an internal goal in the goal section (Fig. 4-2). If this section is not declared (i.e., by having the word goal against the left margin), then the dialog window appears and you can type in goals manually. There is one significant difference. For external goals it is assumed that you want to see the results and they are automatically displayed on the screen. The way internal goals display results, however, must be specified. Also, the goal is satisfied only once *unless* you have told the program to backtrack and give you all the possible solutions.

Chapter 5

Getting Started

YOU'VE INSTALLED YOUR PROGRAM AND ARE READY TO GO. FIRST we'll look at the keyboard and discuss how it will affect the program.

KEYBOARDS

Turbo Prolog assumes that you are using a keyboard layout standard to the IBM PC type of machine. Most keyboards do fall in this pattern, with certain exceptions. The popular Tandy 1000 computers, for example, have twelve function keys in a row above the regular keys instead of ten in two columns of five to the left, as in most arrangements.

Machines that are not meant to be IBM PC compatible, but can do so closely enough by emulation to run Turbo Prolog, may have alien and awkward keyboard layouts for Turbo prolog. In these cases, you're going to have to do a little research in your manual to find out which keys are equivalent to the function keys normally labeled F1 - F10.

To avoid confusion, the examples given in this book will be from the viewpoint of the IBM standard—although occasionally the odd useful note on various other configurations will be given as an aside.

The function keys are labeled F1 - F10 and usually are defined by the particular software currently in control of your computer. In the case of Turbo Prolog, all ten keys perform specific commands, discussed at length in the chapter on the built-in editor. Nonstandard keyboards may sometimes have these keys located in a different place, or they might not be there at all, and you will have to figure an equivalent method of performing the command. Turbo Prolog lends itself to these compromises by providing methods of redefining key functions.

A few other keys will be consistently useful to you as well. The first of these is the Control or (as it is labeled) Ctrl key. Under Turbo prolog, this key is often used to double the capacity of some other key. For example, pressing Ctrl and the left arrow or right arrow key will make them operate like Page Left and Page Right keys instead of just moving one character at a time.

Another keyboard double-up involves the scroll lock, located on the extreme right top of your keyboard. If you look down on the side of this key, you will probably see the word "Break" as well. This, when hit together with the Ctrl key, is a panic stop for long operations. For example, if a program appears to be locked up or looping endlessly, this is the way to stop it.

Don't think of the keyboard as some static thing, with the keys always rigidly taking on the same identity. There are a number of programs called "keyboard enhancers" which will change your keys for increased efficiency. The manufacturer of Turbo Prolog, for example, makes one called SuperKey (Fig. 5-1) that works quite nicely. There are several others, as well.

The Alt of Alternate Key is one that can work in conjunction with all the others, giving you literally dozens of possibilities. Defining these keys is not limited to just a single character either, they can be entire names of products, customers, addresses, or any combination of text and/or numbers that you repeatedly type—such as predicates in Turbo Prolog programs.

Turbo Prolog itself may be used to define keys. In fact, the programs you turn out can be made much slicker and easier to use via key redefinition.

THE MAIN SCREEN

The main screen consists of four separate windows, a menu bar at the top, and an information line at the bottom (Fig. 5-2). From now on when we discuss the "main screen," it is this crucial part of the programming environment that we refer to.

- **Windows** are portions of your computer screen that act independently of other portions. Turbo Prolog allows several of these, of varying sizes, colors, and functions. This windowing ability adds dimension not only to the operation of the programming environment, but also to your own programs. Without windows, only one view of, say, program operation can be allowed at once; with them, you can look at the pro-

Fig. 5-1. SuperKey, a keyboard macro utility, is a great productivity enhancer for programmers.

```
|      Run      Compile      Edit      Options      Files      Setup      Quit      |

|------------------- Editor ---------------------| |------------ Dialog ------------|
| Line 1     Col 1     Indent  Insert  EXAMPLO1. | |True                            |
|/* Program 1 */                                 | |Goal: likes(ellen,What).        |
|/*                                              | |What=tennis                     |
|  Enter the goal on page 18 of the manual.      | |1 Solution                      |
|  Some valuable notes are at the bottom         | |Goal:                           |
|  of this program.                              | |                                |
|*/                                              | |                                |
|                                                | |                                |
|domains                                         | |                                |
|   person, activity = symbol                    | |                                |
|                                                | |                                |
|predicates                                      | |                                |
|   likes(person,activity)                       | |                                |
|                                                | |                                |
|------------------- Message --------------------| |------------ Trace -------------|
|Load EXAMPLO9.PRO                               | |                                |
|Load A:çPROLOG.HLP                              | |                                |
|Compiling EXAMPLO1.PRO                          | |                                |
|likes                                           | |                                |
F8:Previous line  F9:Edit  S-F9:View windows  S-F10:Resize window  Esc:Stop exec
```

Fig. 5-2. The various windows of the Turbo Prolog programming environment offer real ease in development, interactive experimentation, and debugging.

gram listing, the run window, a trace window, and any other information that might be beneficial in debugging a piece of software.

The four windows on the main screen are built into Turbo Prolog and have been customized to assist you with editing, querying, tracing, and debugging. You always have the option of moving, reducing, or enlarging each window. With Version 1.1 of Turbo Prolog you can even use the key combination Ctrl-F10 while any window is active to toggle the window size between its current size and the full screen.

The **editor window**, on the upper left of the main screen and the largest of the four windows, is the one you will use the most. Here you will type all your programs, modify them, and debug them. This window (like the other three) can be expanded to fill the screen as shown in Fig. 5-3.

There are five features of the editor window with which you need to be familiar. This very helpful data appears on the line directly below the "Editor" title line.

The information shown on this line is "Line," "Col," "Indent," "Insert," and (initially) "WORK.PRO." In Version 1.0, the words "Text" and "Free" appear in place of "Line" and "Col." They showed, respectively, the number of characters in the program file and the amount of space still available (maximum of 64K).

```
|      Run       Compile       Edit       Options       Files       Setup       Quit     |

------------------------------------ Editor -----------------------------------------------
|  Line 1       Col 1       Indent   Insert   ANS08.PRO
|/* Answer to exercise on Page 8 */
|/*
|  This is the first example.  Note
|  it has been changed a little but
|  works the same. Look at the WRITE
|  & WRITEF. The slash star (/*)
|  starts a comment and star slash (*/)
|  ends a comment.  NOTE: variables
|  start with capital letters.
|*/
|
|predicates
|    hello
|
|goal
|    hello.
|
|clauses
Use first letter of option  or  select with  ->  or  <-
```

Fig. 5-3. The editor window in the Turbo Prolog environment may be expanded to fill the whole screen, if necessary.

"Line" indicates the line number of the current cursor location; line numbering logically runs from "1" at the top of the file. "Column" refers to the position in a line, as measured from the left margin, where the cursor rests. Line width can be more than the normal 80 columns of screen display, with the screen scrolling horizontally to show you an 80-column view. Thus, if the cursor were 10 characters from the left on the ninth line down from the beginning, the indications would be "Line 9" and "Col 10."

"Indent" indicates that automatic indentation is in effect, about which we shall see more in a later chapter. Programs are easier to read if the various parts are indented by varying amounts from the left margin. If Indent is turned off, lines start at column 1, flush against the left margin.

Fourth on this line is "Insert", which refers to the state of the editor. This simply means that if you move the cursor to a certain point and hit a letter key, that particular letter will be inserted, moving existing text over to make room. The insert state may be toggled off and on by depressing the Ins key. When this is done, the Overwrite indicator replaces Insert. Instead of moving text over, the text is replaced. Both modes are useful.

The last indicator, is moderately obvious: it is the name of the program file currently being edited. Loading other programs into the editor will cause this name to change.

The **dialog window** is to the left of the editor window. A dialog is conversation. This window is where you can "talk" to a Prolog program while it is in operation.

The dialog window will appear if either of two conditions are in force. If you have not specified a goal internally in your program, the window will appear in the upper right quadrant of your screen with the prompt **Goal:** inside it. Enter whatever is appropriate to the program.

The other condition occurs when you have included an internal goal and the program needs information from the operator, but you have not used windowing predicates to create your own window. In the dialog window it might ask "What state do you want the capital of?" You would type **North Carolina** and the answer, **Raleigh**, would pop up, also in the dialog window.

Unless you specifically instruct it otherwise in your program, Turbo Prolog programs will interface with humans through the dialog window. This is true for the programming environment only. When the program is compiled, the output and input will be on the screen as a BASIC program.

The **message window** is down in the lower left of the main screen. As the name implies, this is where Turbo Prolog sends messages to you. During compilation of a program, each step of the process is detailed here for you. If an error occurs, the error message is displayed here.

The various error messages that Turbo prolog will display in the manner are listed in the back of your *Owner's Handbook*.

The **trace window**, located in the lower right of the main programming environment screen, is used to help you find a discrepancy in logic and mend it. It will show what happens as each step is executed.

When you have Turbo Prolog in trace mode, accomplished by typing in the word **trace** on the first line of your program file, you can run the program step by step with the cursor in the editor window following along on each line being executed; meanwhile, in the trace window you are informed of each action as it happens.

Access to compiling and the other major areas of the Turbo Prolog programming environment is achieved from the **menu bar**. When Prolog is first invoked, the title screen appears. Hitting the space bar then gives you the main area with the four windows discussed above and the line of choices along the top.

This arrangement is a convenient method of giving you quick and easy control over the programming environment. Each choice, like moving down a pyramid, is a gateway to several other choices, all of which lead yet to others.

At the top of the main screen, along the menu bar, there are seven main choices: "Run", "Compile", "Edit", "Options", "Files", "Setup", and "Quit."

Making a menu choice, on the main menu bar or in one of the submenus, may be done in two ways. The first is to use the first letter of the choice. To access the Options menu, for example, it is only necessary to type *the letter* "O" or "o." Turbo Prolog is not case-sensitive here, so either upper- or lowercase entries are allowed.

The second method of accessing choices on the menu bar is to use the directional cursor keys, i.e., the arrow keys on your numeric keypad. On the main menu bar, you use the left and right keys to highlight the desired choice and then hit Return to execute. In a submenu, since the choices are listed vertically, the up and down keys are employed in the same manner.

The Esc (escape) key is used to abort from a submenu back to the next higher one. Since the menu bar cannot be accessed when you are in a window, hitting the Escape key will return you to a place in the program where a letter or arrow movement will let a menu option be selected.

The **options menu** allows you four choices, all related to compilation. It is accessed by typing the letter O or by using the horizontal arrow keys to highlight the word "Options" and then hitting the Return key.

The first choice on the Options menu, "Memory," is the one you will use the most. This compiles the program within your working memory and, assuming all is correct, gives you immediate operation. The program is stored there until you compile another or exit Turbo Prolog. You can run the program over and over without having to go through the sometimes moderately lengthy compilation process each time.

The Memory option is much like using a BASIC interpreter in this respect. You get interaction during programming, and you can try out a number of things until you find the best mode of operation. Only then do you compile a finished result to disk. The following choices in the Options submenu concern that.

The second choice, "OBJ file," places your program into a binary file but does not link it (set it up to be run independently). You can exit to your operating system and use an external linker like the one supplied with MS-DOS or PC-DOS from Microsoft (Version 2.14 or later) or PLINK86 Version 1.48 overlay linker from Phoenix S.A. The primary reason for this facility is the possibility that there might not be room enough to compile the program while Turbo Prolog is itself resident in your computer's working memory. If you have the minimum required memory of 384K, this may happen often.

Next is the "EXE (auto link)" option. This will cause your program—when it has been chosen previously—to be compiled into a stand-alone program when Compile is chosen from the main menu bar. Version 1.0 of Turbo Prolog uses a finesse method through DOS batch files to invoke Microsoft's linker (LINK.EXE) to accomplish this; this means you must make sure LINK.EXE (Version 2.14 or greater) is present or in a DOS path that will allow it to be found by the compiling process. Version 1.1 of Turbo Prolog has its own built-in linker, which has the added benefit of generating slightly smaller EXE programs.

The last option, "PROJECT (all modules)," has been added to Version 1.1 and allows programs to be written in small, easier-to-understand chunks. All of these can then be joined together during compilation. You may also develop and use a series of standard modules, thus speeding up development time.

Now it is possible to automatically compile all modules in a project. Select Compile Project under the Options pull-down menu, give the name of the project, select the Compile option, and all the modules will be compiled. The Prolog modules should reside in the PRO directory, and the .PRJ file should reside on the .OBJ directory.

By choosing "F" on the main menu bar, the **file management** submenu appears and you have a number of choices. Many of the functions here are the same ones you would be using outside of Turbo Prolog in your disk operating system, a mark of convenience. If you *do* need to exit temporarily, however, one of the choices in this submenu lets you do that and return with everything just as it was before, including the same file still loaded into the editor window.

The choices under Files are very helpful (Figs. 5-4 and 5-5). You can get a listing of files in the current directory, print a file out on paper, save a file to disk, change directories, load a program, copy one file to another, rename files, find the name of the current program file, obtain

```
    Run      Compile      Edit      Options      Files      Setup      Quit

------------------------------------ Editor ---|Load
 Line 1     Col 1     Indent   Inser
/*  Answer to first exercise on Page|Directory: B:çprograms
/*                                  |File mask: *.PRO
  numlist (i(1,  -------------- Directory: B:çPROGRAMS\*.PRO ---------------
                | DIFF.PRO      D_CURVE.PRO     GENI.PRO       HANOI.PRO
                | LTEST.PRO     MENU.PRO        QSORT.PRO      SANAL.PRO
                |
                |
                |
  This is an exa|
  declarations  |
*/              |
                |
domains
    integerlist = i(integer,integerlist) ; null

predicates
    numlist(integerlist)

PgUp,PgDn and <-,->:Move cursor   S-F10:Resize window   Esc:End
```

*Fig. 5-4. You can view directories and the files within them via pop-down windows. The "file mask" *.PRO shows only those files with PRO extensions.*

```
   Run       Compile      Edit      Options      Files      Setup      Quit

               Editor                          |Load               |g
 Line 1      Col 1      Indent   Inser
                                   |Directory: A:\                    |
                                   |                                  |

                                           |Rename              |
                                           |File Name           |
                                           |Module list         |
                                           |Zap file in editor  |
                                           |Erase               |
                                           |Operating system    |

                                                       Trace

Use first letter of option  or  select with  ->  or  <-
```

Fig. 5-5. In Turbo Prolog the file handling features are useful indeed.

a list of modules for your current project, zap (remove) the file in the editor window, and exit to the operating system with the option of returning without having to restart Turbo Prolog. A neat feature of these file manipulation facilities is a *mask* that will allow Turbo Prolog to see only Prolog program files instead of all the clutter you might otherwise have to contend with.

Another very useful feature can be used when you wish to load a file but do not remember its name. Hitting the Return key gets you a listing of the currently selected directory. You may then use the cursor keys to move up and down through the directory. As you do so, the file selected will be highlighted. When the one you want is indicated, merely tap the Return key and it will be loaded into the editor window, ready to be worked on.

On the Files menu there is also a selection that lets you go to your operating system environment and use it as a *shell.* It's labeled "Operating system" and is selected either by the arrow keys or pressing the letter O. You are dropped into DOS and may perform any commands necessary here; then typing "EXIT" will return you to Prolog.

The other choices allow you to print a hard copy of the program in the editor window or any other file ("Print"), copy files on disk ("Copy"), rename files ("Rename"), give you a list of modules present ("Module list"), remove the current program ("Zap"), and erase a file ("Erase").

Choosing **Edit**, either with the arrow keys and highlighting or via typing an E, puts you into the editor window, where you can input and modify your programs. The next chapter is concerned with operating Turbo Prolog's powerful built-in editor.

The **Run** option causes the program currently in the editor window to be compiled to memory and, if no mistakes are found, to run. If mistakes are detected, you will get the appropriate error message in the message window. Then you may either use the editor to correct the syntax mistake or the trace facilities to determine where the logic of the program breaks down.

When the **compile** option is selected, Turbo Prolog compiles the current program using whatever criteria that has been previously selected using the Options submenu. Using this selection in conjunction with the .EXE or .OBJ options lets you create stand-alone programs.

The **Quit** option is pretty obvious. Choosing the Quit option causes Turbo prolog to tidy up everything and return control of your computer to the disk operating system. The one thing you want to make sure of, during this process, is that any file you may have active in the editor window is saved to disk; otherwise your changes will be lost. Turbo Prolog will help you to remember this by asking "Save old text (y/n):" if the file has been modified since being loaded in or created.

That brings us to the remaining selection on the menu bar, the one that allows you to customize the Turbo Prolog programming environment to your own needs.

The submenu accessed by selecting **Setup**, gives you the facilities needed to look at and temporarily or permanently change the configuration of the Turbo Prolog programming environment.

You may rearrange, change colors, and generally play with the configuration of the edit, dialog, trace, and message windows to your heart's content. It is a quick and easy process using the Setup pull-down menus. You can even save configurations automatically to the PROLOG.SYS file, so that the next time you activate the system the desired window layout will appear. Or you may save any number of configurations to files with other names—calling them whenever a particular job or situation warrants them.

In the Setup submenu we have several other submenus, giving you access to choices another level down. The selections here are "Colors," "Window size," "Directories," "Miscellaneous settings," "Load configuration," and "Save configuration." As in all other submenus, you may choose the one you want by either typing its first letter, or by using the up and down arrow keys on your computer's numeric keypad to highlight the choice, and then execute it by hitting the Return key.

The first of these choices, the **Colors** submenu, lets you set the colors of the various windows. This may either be a temporary or a permanent change, depending on whether or not you save the changes to a configuration file. You may have any number of different configurations stored on your hard disk or on regular floppies.

Choose this submenu of the Setup submenu and take a look at it. The choices are "Edit window," "Message window," "Trace window," "Aux edit window," "Pull down window," and "Status line." Each selection changes the color of the window associated with it. The "Pull down window" may not be immediately obvious to you—this is the menu bar and the various submenu windows that pop down.

Changing colors is simple. Choose the window whose color setup you want to modify. Instructions appear on the bottom line of your screen. All you have to do is use the left and right arrow keys to change the background color, and tap the up and down arrows to scroll through the letter colors. As you do these operations, it is reflected in the colors shown in the window under modification. A tip here: Type something into the editor window before you go to change it. It is a bit hard to guess at text colors when there is nothing there.

While this process is in progress, on the status line at the bottom of your screen something appears, like "Attr= 23." This means the screen attribute. Using this, you can calculate not only the foreground and background colors of the programming environment screens, but also the colors of windows in your finished programs.

Essentially each color has a foreground and background *attribute.* You simply choose the ones you want and add them together. For example, green has a foreground attribute of 2 and red has a background attribute of 64. Thus, if you wanted a screen of green on red, you would add the two together and use a screen attribute of 66.

Hitting any other key besides the arrow keys will return you to the "Colors" submenu. The Esc key will back you up through the submenus until the main menu bar is reached.

Hint: Take the most pains with the editor screen. You will be looking at it the most, so make it easy on the old eyeballs; if you have a burning sensation in your eyes after a day of programming, you have a bad setup. What I've finally settled on for both my word processing screen and Turbo Prolog editing screen is blue on white.

Once you have completed setting the colors in all of the five windows and on the status line, hit the Esc key and you will return to the Setup submenu. Note: None of these changes are permanent yet, so if you were to leave Turbo Prolog now, all your color settings would be lost. We will see how to make the change permanent shortly.

The next selection in the Setup submenu lets you set the sizes of the four windows—editor, dialog, trace, and message—in the Turbo Prolog programming environment. As with colors, this can be a temporary or a permanent change depending on whether you save the changes to a configuration file. You may have any number of different configurations stored on your hard disk or on regular floppies.

Choose this submenu of the "Setup" submenu and take a look at it. The first four choices are "Editor window," "Dialog window," "Message window," and "Trace window." The last choice, "Aux edit window," may not be quite so obvious. The auxiliary editor window is opened from inside the editor window. One of its major functions is to allow two program files to be open at once; this is valuable in long programs where a series of predicates that you may have already worked out for another program would work well in your current one. Using the "Aux edit" window, you can open the old file and copy the necessary chunks of it into the current one, thus saving much typing.

Window sizing, like color changing, is a simple process in the Turbo Prolog programming environment. Pick the window you want to resize on the submenu. Now look down at the status line on the bottom of the screen. As it was with colors, the necessary commands are noted there for your convenience. All you have to do is to use the arrow keys to change the window's size; pressing the Ctrl and arrow keys at the same time will make the resizing occur in larger increments. Using the shift and the arrow keys together will move the window around on the screen.

If you make a window too narrow, you still will not lose any data. It will either be continued on the next line of the window or out of sight to the right. Entering that window and using the cursor keys to move around in it will display all the information. Many times it is not necessary to see, for example, the trace window. You are only concerned with it in extensive debugging of a program.

The hot tip here is to make largest the window that you use the most. That's the editor window. In fact, in my own setup I have resized my editor window until it covers the whole screen. Nothing lost by doing this—the dialog window, for example, appears automatically whenever I run a program that calls for it—and I gain much convenience and ease of reading program listings.

You are allowed to change the window size settings as many times during the course of a programming session as pleases you. These changes are temporary so far, and the window setup in your permanent configuration file is the one to which Turbo Prolog reverts when you exit and then restart.

Turbo prolog must know where you want files stored and where to look for them when you issue a call. To set these, you choose the **Directories** selection from the Setup submenu. You may, of course, enter the full pathname of a file each time, but when your directory tree starts growing branches, it becomes hard to remember all of them—not to mention the tedium of all that typing.

Using the Directories choice, you can look at and change whatever the current default directory and drive specifications might be. There are four of these: "PRO directory," "OBJ directory," "EXE directory," and "Turbo directory."

The PRO directory is the one that is used for all the file handling in the Files submenu. The name refers to the .PRO extension to filenames that tells Turbo Prolog that this file is a Prolog program. The preset default setting for all four of them is "A:\" or the primary drive on your computer. If you have a hard disk, the first thing you want to do is change this to directory C:\ *plus* the name of the subdirectory in which your programs will reside.

If you have a directory for Turbo Prolog, you may very well call it "PROLOG." One solution would then be to create a subdirectory of this for your programs and name it "PROGRAMS." To tell Turbo prolog where to go for these programs, you would select "PRO directory" in the "Directories" submenu of the submenu and enter **C:\PROLOG\PROGRAMS**, the complete path that your computer needs to find that particular directory on the hard disk.

The same goes for the other selections on this submenu. "OBJ directory" lets you specify where object files and .PRJ (project) files are stored; both are types of files involved in compiling programs. The ".EXE directory" is also connected with compilation, and is a place where Turbo Prolog will put the finished executable stand-alone program for you.

The "Turbo directory" tells the system where all the files needed for the operation of the programming environment are currently residing. These include the files PROLOG.EXE (the actual Turbo Prolog program), PROLOG.ERR, PROLOG.HLP, PROLOG.LIB, PROLOG.SYS, and all other files with the .SYS extension. The last, by the way, designates a file that stores all the parameters for window sizes, colors, directories, and so forth. You can have as many of these as you can cram onto disks.

The **miscellaneous settings** submenu has three choices, two of which can be especially significant in compiling programs because they affect the amount of working memory in your computer that is allocated for use by Turbo Prolog.

First, however, the other choice. "IBM-CGA Adapter" is the top selection on this submenu. "CGA" means "Color Graphics Adapter." This selection is a toggle to turn the CGA adapter on or off. Your choice is simple: If you have this board installed in your computer, turn it on. Hitting the Return key will cause this feature to be toggled off and on, with the word OFF or ON appearing to tell you which state it's in. That's all there is to it.

The second of the three choices is "Auto load message." Like the CGA adapter selection, this one is also an on/off toggle. If it is on, *all* the Turbo Prolog error messages are loaded into memory when you call it up from DOS to begin a programming session. When an error occurs in one of your programs, the error message is immediately available. This speeds things up by making it unnecessary for Prolog to hunt for PROLOG.ERR, the error messages file. Also it means you do not have to keep that particular disk in the drive.

It is the compilation process which sometimes requires all the possible room in your working memory that you can allow. This is when turning the "Auto load" message feature off becomes important. I just checked to see how much memory is involved here. Using Version 1.1 of Turbo Prolog, I find that with Auto load on it takes up 246,704 bytes of memory. Turning it off and reloading Turbo Prolog shows that only 239,056 is used—almost a 7K savings. Not much, you might think now, but it could mean being able to keep some of your memory-resident utilities. Besides, the faster access times and greater storage space of hard disks can really afford the tradeoff of slightly longer time for error messages, versus more working memory. If you have a hard disk, I recommend leaving "Auto load" off.

The last selection on the miscellaneous settings submenu, "Stack size," has an even more dramatic effect on memory use. The *stack* is that part of your memory that Turbo prolog reserves to use for parameter transfer. The default size is 600 *paragraphs*, each of which is 16 bytes long, for a total of 9600 bytes. This is the lower limit, the minimum needed for proper operation. The upper limit is 4000 paragraphs or 64K (called a memory *segment* in IBM terminology). A quick bit of subtraction tells us that there is a range here of 54.4K for you to play with, which is a significant percentage of your computer's memory if you have 384K.

I can make no suggestion here for the best stack size setting; it depends on the particular type of program with which you are working. We'll discuss this further when we look at program design considerations. The only recommendation I can make is to do what I did: leave it set on 600 and whenever you get a "stack overflow" error message, reset it temporarily to a higher value, experimenting to find the smallest value that will still work.

Finally, here's how to load and save configurations of various window sizes, colors, directory paths, and the three settings for graphics, "Auto load" messages, and stack size, that we just covered. The last two choices on the Setup submenu are concerned with this: "Load Configuration" and "Save Configuration." Let's take them in the more logical, reverse, order.

When you first begin experimenting in the Turbo Prolog programming environment, you will want to customize it to your general needs: color, window sizes, and so on. The changes are all temporary settings; if you turned off your computer right now, they would all be lost. To make them permanent, select the "Save configuration" option on the Setup menu. You will be asked for a name. The default configuration is PROLOG.SYS, and you may choose this one just by hitting the Return key. All of your settings will be then recorded to this file and, whenever Turbo Prolog is initialized, this is the setup that will appear. You can, of course, amend this as often as pleases you.

The initial setup out of the way, you now can consider specialized screen configurations for various types of jobs. You might have one for tracing and another for editing and yet another for running programs from inside the programming environment. You can have as many as you want, just as long as they have unique names if stored on the same disk. For the examples in this paragraph, you might call them TRACE.SYS, EDITOR.SYS, and RUN.SYS. You could just as well name them BILL.SYS, MARVIN.SYS, and SUSIE_Q.SYS—whatever you can remember most easily.

When Turbo Prolog first comes on, PROLOG.SYS is automatically consulted to set up the screen configuration. If you want to load in another of your recorded configurations, you could come again to this submenu and type in the name of the new file. This configuration would stay until you loaded in another. Again, you may also make only temporary changes using the various options on the Setup submenu; it is not necessary that they be in a file.

Not that you are very familiar with the programming environment and itching to do some more practical stuff, let's move on to where you will be spending the most time—the editor window!

Chapter 6

The Editor

THIS CHAPTER WILL HELP YOU GAIN PROFICIENCY WITH TURBO Prolog's built-in editor. If you are already familiar with word processing programs such as WordStar and MultiMate, or the editing functions built into integrated software like SideKick and the programming environment of Turbo Pascal, you will find the editor here to be an old friend. If not, you will find it easy to learn and use.

Turbo Prolog programs, like most computer programs these days, begin with a programmer typing lines of instructions into the computer. The later steps of compiling and even tracing malfunctioning programs are pretty much automatic.

Entering and editing command lines is word processing. Right now you need, not a programming language, but a full-featured screen editor to make the job of getting the programs typed in easier. In fact, the editor included as part of the programming environment really lets you quickly enter and modify programs, run them, and then add refinements—all in the editor mode (Fig. 6-1).

A word processing program lets you add, delete, move, and copy what is still essentially text. Earlier programming languages either expected you to provide external word processing or program editor software or, at best, provided a few rudimentary commands built into their programming environment.

Turbo Prolog's editor is fully integrated with the rest of the programming system. This means ease in entering and modifying programs. If

```
|    Run     Compile     Edit     Options     Files     Setup     Quit    |

------------- Editor ---------------   --|TURBO PROLOG version 1.1 |
| Line 1    Col 1    Indent  Insert  WORK.PRO ||  |---------------------------||
|                                             ||  |Colors                     ||
|                                             ||  |Window size                ||
|                                             ||  |Dire ----------------      ||
|                                             ||  |Misc |Edit      window |   ||
|                                             ||  |Load |Dialog    window |   ||
|                                             ||  |Save |Message   window |   ||
|                                             ||  ------|Trace     window |----|
|                                             ||        |Aux edit  window |    |
|                                             ||        -------------------    |
|                                             ||                               |
|                                             ||                               |
|                                             ||                               |

------------- Message ---------------   ---------- Trace ----------
|                                             ||                               |
|Compiling WORK.PRO                           ||                               |
|Compilation successful                       ||                               |
|                                             ||                               |

Use first letter of option  or  select with  ->  or  <-
```

Fig. 6-1. Window size may be set via a submenu of the Setup menu.

an error occurs during compile or run time, for example, control is automatically returned to the editor *at the point in the program where it bombed.* This error-triggered automatic switching is so fast that you will forget the system is a compiler instead of an interpreter. The error-checking facility is superior to that of most Prolog interpreters. It finds and points out problems, such as a variable being used only once, that other systems require a separate "lint" program to achieve.

The Turbo Prolog "trace" mode lets you run the program step by step, with the cursor in the editor window following each line being executed; in the trace window you are continually informed of the action currently taking place. It's a great aid, and a real breakthrough in Prolog programming. The combination of moving source code and trace window operational monitoring clearly shows logic and makes finding miscues a breeze.

The editor is a superset of the one included with Borland's popular Turbo Pascal system. It uses easy-to-comprehend WordStar-like commands. These commands include an extensive set of key combinations to position the cursor, scrolling, searching, line insert and delete, and block manipulations such as mark, copy, move, and delete.

That's not all! The editor itself can access other files, i.e., to edit more than one at a time. What's more, you can move sections of program from one file to another. The only limit is that while you can have more than one file open at a time, you can only see two of them. Each auxiliary editor window opened overlies the previous one, but it is merely a matter of closing the most recent window to get back to the previous one. The main editor window is always available.

IN AND OUT OF THE EDITOR

Activating the editor is simple. Once you have started Turbo Prolog hitting the space bar gives you the main screen. Like all of Turbo Prolog's menus, there are two ways you can select the Edit option from the main menu bar and invoke the editor. The easiest is simply to tap the E key. The cursor will immediately move down into the editor window, showing you that the editor is now active, ready for your input. The second way is to use the left and right arrow keys until the word "Edit" is highlighted. Then hit Return and you will be in the editor window.

Leaving the editor is just as easy. Simply tap the Esc key and you will be deposited back on the menu bar. Whatever you have entered in the editor window will remain there. You still will be able to see it, but if you quit Turbo Prolog without saving that file, any changes you made will be lost. To save a file, choose Files from the menu bar and then the Save option from the submenu that pops down. You may also use the Zap option to remove the file completely from the editor, in effect discarding whatever was there.

Turbo Prolog offers on-line help from within the editor window (Fig. 6-2). By hitting the F1 function key, a help window, which temporarily overlays the material on your screen, can be accessed. When the key is pressed a "main menu" pops up, its position depending on where your cursor is located in the editor window. This is not to be confused with the main menu bar; it is merely a vertical submenu. The first choice on

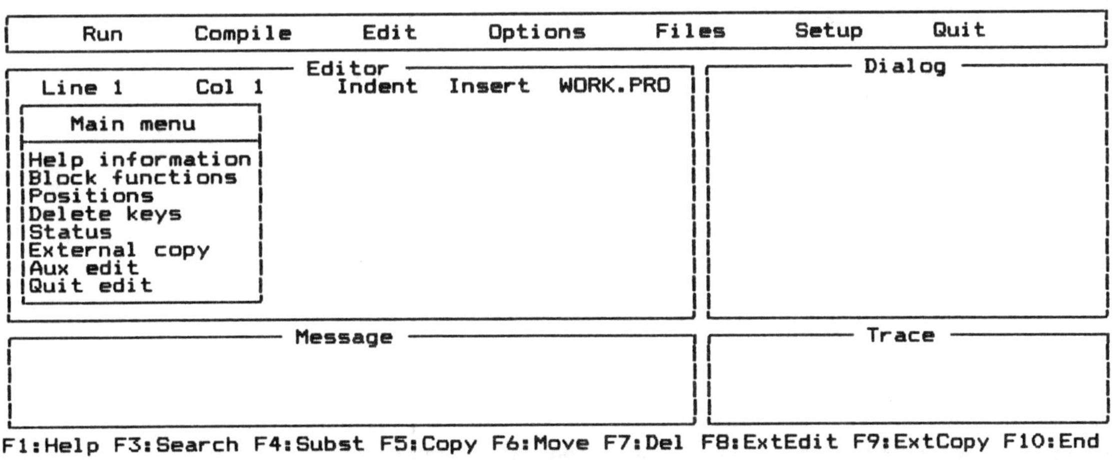

Fig. 6-2. On-screen help is available by pressing the F1 function key when working in the editor window.

this submenu is Help Information. That selection will be already highlighted when the menu appears, so just punch your Return key to activate it.

This information is not extensive help by any means, nor is it context-sensitive; the help messages do not vary with the particular operation you happen to be engaged in. It is simply an electronic "cheat sheet" to help you remember various commands. You move up and down through it using the standard scheme of up and down arrow and PgUp and PgDn keys. Hitting F10 or the Esc key will cause the help window to evaporate and return you to exactly where you were.

The help information covers subjects you'll need in programming. The function key assignments are what you see when the help screen appears. Paging downward shows editor commands next. The editor commands cover positioning, block moves and copies, deleting and inserting functions, and the others that we will be covering in this chapter.

The help file (PROLOG.HLP) is a text file that you can edit to add whatever information you think will help you. In fact, you can even use Turbo Prolog's own built-in editor to make these additions. Here's how.

From the main menu bar, select the Files submenu, then the Load choice. When you are asked for a name, enter **PROLOG.HLP**. The top few lines of that file will appear in the editor window and the Files submenu will disappear. You may then select Edit and add your notes and clarifications.

When you are through, exit the edit window, access Files again, and save the new help file. It is not necessary to type in **PROLOG.HLP** when doing this; just hit Return, because Turbo Prolog knows which file you were working on. Then choose the Zap option on Files and clear out your editor window.

If you do not own a separate word processing program, this built-in editor makes a quite passable one. You can even write letters with it, printing the files out when you are finished.

PREPARING TO EDIT

First, before entering the editor window, either clear it or make sure the program or other file to be edited is loaded.

The file and directory manipulating functions in the Files pull-down submenu on the main menu bar are used to fetch files from disk and put them in the editor window. The Load selection is the one you will probably use the most. Once this is engaged, you will be asked for a file name. It is not necessary to enter an actual name here as long as there are some Prolog program files (i.e., those having the .PRO extension). Just hit the Return key and a window showing the Prolog files available will pop up. Use the arrow keys to select the one you want and press Return once more. The file will then be loaded into the editor window.

If you wish to start a new file, all you have to do is make sure the editor window is clear. If something is still in it, either save it to disk and then Zap it off the screen, or dump it by simply using the Zap choice.

The next step, in either case, is simply to choose the Edit option from the main menu bar and watch the cursor magically appear inside the edit window. Begin to edit.

The Turbo Prolog editor is just like a typewriter, except it's a lot simpler to use. If you hit the wrong letter, press the backspace key, and the mistake is automatically blanked out and you can type in a new letter.

The cursor—that blinking bar that points to your place in the program or document—stays one space in front, pointing at the next place where a letter or number goes.

This is the easiest way to add things to the file you are editing. There are other ways too, some of them much quicker and much more powerful. These include copying blocks of text, importing large chunks from other program files, and of course loading in files from disk (Fig. 6-3). We'll look at these in a moment, but on with the fundamentals of the editor.

Deleting Text

There are several ways to remove unwanted text (Fig. 6-4). The first two methods involve taking out a character. The backspace key we just met. There is also the Del key. This key, too, removes one character

```
     Run     Compile     Edit     Options     Files     Setup     Quit

              Editor                               Dialog
 Line 1     Col 1     Indent  Insert  EXAMPLO1.

  Block functions
                    page 18 of the manual.
   F3: Search text  s are at the bottom
 S-F3: Search again
   F4: Replace text
 S-F4: Replace again
   F5: Copy block
 S-F5: Copy again   = symbol
   F6: Move block
 S-F6: Move again
   F7: Remove block vity)
     Main menu
                                                    Trace
    likes(ellen,tennis).
    likes(john,football).
    likes(tom,baseball).
    likes(eric,swimming).

F1:Help F3:Search F4:Subst F5:Copy F6:Move F7:Del F8:ExtEdit F9:ExtCopy F10:End
```

Fig. 6-3. Block operations may be executed in the editor via WordStar-like commands, function keys, or this pop-down menu.

```
     Run      Compile      Edit      Options      Files      Setup      Quit

 ─────────────────── Editor ──────────────────── ─────────── Dialog ───────────
  Line 1      Col 1      Indent  Insert  EXAMPLO1.
 ┌──────────────────────────┐
 │        Delete keys       │
 ├──────────────────────────┤of the manual.
 │Ctrl BS: Del line         │ the bottom
 │Ctrl QY: Del to end of line│
 │Del    : Del char         │
 │BS     : Del char to left │
 │        Main menu         │
 └──────────────────────────┘

 predicates
     likes(person,activity)

 clauses                                          ─────────── Trace ────────────
     likes(ellen,tennis).
     likes(john,football).
     likes(tom,baseball).
     likes(eric,swimming).

F1:Help F3:Search F4:Subst F5:Copy F6:Move F7:Del F8:ExtEdit F9:ExtCopy F10:End
```

Fig. 6-4. Various means of deleting text also are available as pop-downs.

at a time. There is no redundancy here, however, because they do it differently. This difference is that the Del key removes character and space; the backspace key simply erases the character. You will soon find yourself using one or the other, depending on the situation. It also is important that you be aware of how these two keys work in the programs you write.

Saving and Backup

As you edit a file, it is constantly saved in your computer's RAM. This is not the most secure place for your hard work to reside for any appreciable time. Regular saving of your program to disk, about every 15 minutes, is one of the most important habits you will ever develop.

Remember, the program is saved by exiting the editor window and using the arrow keys to select the Save feature in the Files submenu. The name of the file you are working on will automatically be there and you can just hit the Return key. If you want to save it under a different name, you are allowed to specify the new name at that time.

File names are limited to eight characters, letters, or numbers, plus a three-letter extension. Spaces and special characters, with the exception of the underline character, are not allowed; the MS-DOS operating system imposes these restrictions, not this software. Turbo Prolog, however, does want you to add an extension of .PRO for a program file, and other extensions such as .OBJ and .EXE for other types of files.

The Cursor

As you know, the cursor points to your place in the text. There are other ways to move the cursor than just one letter at a time, which will become important to you (Fig. 6-5).

One way the cursor is moved is by hitting the Return key. This will cause it to drop down a line and pop all the way back over to the left-hand margin, exactly analogous to punching the carriage return on a typewriter.

Basic cursor movement is accomplished by using the arrow keys. There is an up, down, left, and right arrow key.

The Pg Up and Pg Dn keys cause the text to move up or down one screen page. The number of lines this involves depends upon what vertical size at which you have the window set. The Home and End keys cause movement to the beginning of a line or the end of a line, respectively. Go ahead and load one of the longer example files or the help file (PROLOG.HLP) and experiment with cursor control.

Command Key Combinations

Specifically to the topic we are on now—editing—Borland made another in their long line of canny moves. They chose to use similar, often the *same* commands that MicroPro International's WordStar word processing program uses (Fig. 6-6).

```
|      Run      Compile      Edit      Options      Files      Setup      Quit      |

------------------------ Editor ------------------------  ------------ Dialog ------------
| Line 1      Col 1      Indent  Insert  EXAMPL01. ||                                    |
||                                                 ||                                    |
||        Positions        |                       ||                                    |
||-------------------------| 18 of the manual.     ||                                    |
||Ctrl PgUp: Start text    |e at the bottom        ||                                    |
||Ctrl PgDn: End text      |                       ||                                    |
||Home     : Start line     |                       ||                                    |
||End      : End line       |                       ||                                    |
||PgUp     : Page up        |                       ||                                    |
||PgDn     : Page down      |mbol                   ||                                    |
||Ctrl <-- : Word left      |                       ||                                    |
||Ctrl --> : Word right     |                       ||                                    |
||F2       : Go to line     |)                      ||                                    |
||S-F2     : Current line|                          |                                     |
||        Main menu        |                        | ------------ Trace ------------     |
|                                                   ||                                    |
|     likes(john,football).                         ||                                    |
|     likes(tom,baseball).                          ||                                    |
|     likes(eric,swimming).                         ||                                    |

F1:Help F3:Search F4:Subst F5:Copy F6:Move F7:Del F8:ExtEdit F9:ExtCopy F10:End
```

Fig. 6-5. Cursor positioning can be accomplished via menu.

Help

INSERT & DELETE	COMMAND	KEY
Insert mode on/off	Ctrl-V	Ins
Insert line	Ctrl-N	
Delete line	Ctrl-Y	
Delete to end of line	Ctrl-Q-Y	
Delete right word	Ctrl-T	
Delete char under cursor	Ctrl-G	Del
Delete left character	Ctrl-H	
BLOCK COMMANDS	**COMMAND**	**KEY**
Mark block begin	Ctrl-K-B	F7
Mark block end	Ctrl-K-K	F8
Hide/display block	Ctrl-K-H	
Copy block	Ctrl-K-C	
Move block	Ctrl-K-V	
Delete block	Ctrl-K-Y	
Read block from disk	Ctrl-K-R	
Write block to disk	Ctrl-K-W	
Print block	Ctrl-K-P	
MISC. COMMANDS	**COMMAND**	**KEY**

Fig. 6-6. The millions of WordStar users will recognize these commands shown in the Turbo Prolog editor window.

The really significant thing about this is WordStar's widespread, almost generic influence on word processing. With millions of users, WordStar-like commands are understood by many of us—perhaps even you already. This does not mean it's all that good—there are several better, less awkward word processing programs now available. But with the even wider pool of people now familiar with these commands through WordStar, all of its clones, SideKick, and the Turbo Pascal programming environment, it was only logical that the same configuration should apply with the editor in Turbo Prolog. Like I said, "canny." The fact that so many people can easily use the editor increases sales measurably.

Many of the cursor movements in the editor window may be done by using key command combinations. These key commands use control sequences (Fig. 6-7), such as pressing the CTRL, Q, and R keys to cause the cursor to move back to the top of a file. This is done by depressing the CTRL and the Q keys at the same time. The editor will then wait for the R key (or whatever other command you want to give in this series). You can even let up on those two keys; the movement will occur even if you are a hundred or two hundred lines down into the file. The cursor will jerk back to the top and the first lines of text will be displayed in the editor window.

Control sequences can be done also with the Alt and shift keys, and the function keys (F1 - F10) are defined for certain commands. CTRL-E corresponds to the up arrow, CTRL-X to the down arrow and CTRL-S and CTRL-D to the left and right arrow keys respectively. You might find it helpful to print out the portion of the PROLOG.HLP file which deals with command key sequences and keep it handy for reference until you've used the editor enough to memorize the most-used commands.

You may move one character left with CTRL-S or one character right using CTRL-D. To move a word left press CTRL-A and CTRL-F will pop your cursor one word right. To page up one screen "page" at a time you may use CTRL-R or the Pg Up key, while paging down is done either by the key combination or CTRL-C or the Pg Dn key over on the numerical key pad. To go to the left margin on a line either the CTRL-Q-S (three keys) combination or Home key (just one) do the same thing. To go right to the end of a line CTRL-Q-D or the more convenient End key may be employed.

Getting to the top of a screen page may be accomplished either by CTRL-Q-R or CTRL-Home, and to the bottom of the page is done with CTRL-Q-X or CTRL-End. Moving to the top of the file uses the CTRL-Q-R combination or CTRL-PgUp. CTRL-Q-C and CTRL-PgDn take the cursor to the end. CTRL-Q-B moves it to the beginning of a marked block of text, CTRL-Q-K to the end of a text block, and CTRL-Q-P to the last cursor position.

There is a *third* way to do these cursor commands in Turbo Prolog Version 1.1 and higher, by using the "main menu." This menu is not to be confused with the main menu bar along the top of the screen above the programming environment's four windows, but here refers to the pop-up submenu we met when discussing "Help" by tapping the F1 key while inside the editor window. By choosing the "Positions" selection you get another submenu, this one listing all the cursor movements. Just select the one you want by highlighting it and hitting Return, or by typing the first letter of its title. You will be immediately returned to the editor window and that cursor movement is performed. Once you use the "main menu" submenu for a function such as "Positions," the next time you hit F1 it will come up on that submenu and will continue doing so until you choose the "main menu" option and specify another set of functions.

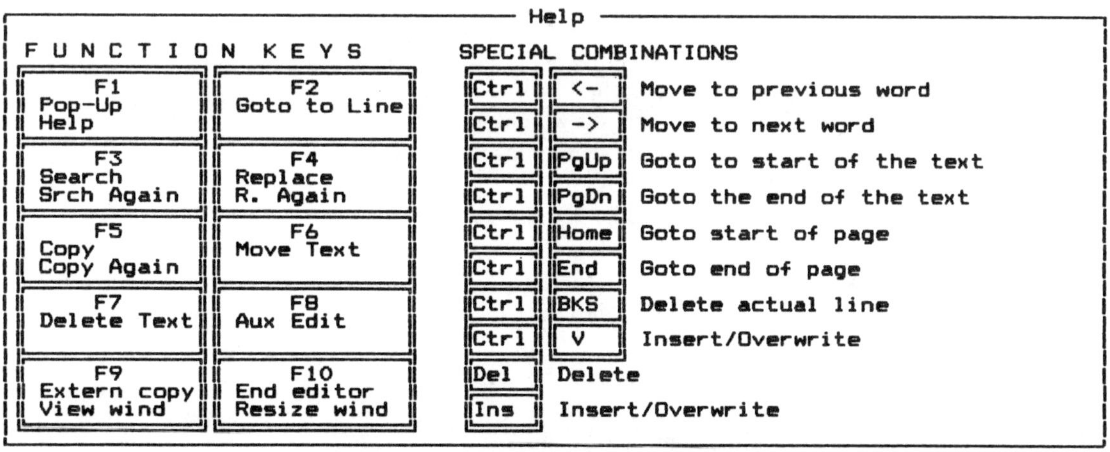

Fig. 6-7. Help screen showing the function key and control key command combinations.

Insertion and Deletion

Insertion and deletion are two of the firm foundations of the word processing concept. The difference between the Del and backspace keys is that the former deletes the character to the immediate left of the cursor, and the latter takes out the character upon which the cursor is blinking. In both cases, any text to the right of the deleted character all gets shifted over one space to the left, closing up the gap.

The editor built into Turbo Prolog gives you several ways to delete larger chunks of text. the biggest are the block delete/move functions.

Deleting a complete line is done with a CTRL-Y key combination. Warning: This removes the line totally no matter where the cursor may be on it. CTRL-Q-Y will delete only that text from the cursor's present position to the end of the line. To delete the *word* to the right of the cursor, use a CTRL-T. These delete commands are also available under the "Delete keys" selection on the pop-up "main menu" submenu.

Insertion is pretty much an automatic process. You can insert large blocks of text using block commands. Basically, however, on the two types of insert states you only have to worry about one command—which may be invoked either with the Ins key, or by using the WordStar-like CTRL-V. This toggles between the insert (the default mode) and the "overwrite." When insert is selected, any text you enter will push everything on the line to its right over and make room for itself. Overwrite, on the other hand, allows you to write over a word without moving the rest of the line. Characters are replaced by the new characters typed over them.

BLOCKS

Blocks are simply a portion of text. A block might include three words or 300 lines, whatever you decide in view of the particular area of your program file that needs to be manipulated. Manipulation might take the form of deleting, moving, or copying the block to some other location.

To use this feature, you must first *mark* the block, that is, tell the editor which part of the words on the screen on which you want it to act. This is done by moving the cursor to the beginning or the end of the block—whichever is closest.

The start of a block is marked with the key combination command CTRL-K-B, or alternatively, with the F7 function. Then move the cursor to the end of the block (or the start, if you are doing it from bottom up). The command CTRL-K-K ends the block definition or, again in the Turbo Prolog editor, the function key F8 also performs this operation. Just remember to use the end mark at the end and the start mark at the start.

As soon as the block commands are entered the block of text changes in intensity, setting it off from the rest of the text on the screen. You may now choose from several manipulations. You might want to delete it: merely hit F7, or the key combination CTRL-K-Y.

The block delete command is sensitive; just an accidental brush on the F7 key could cause your block to evaporate instantly. A method is provided to leave the block defined but have it on "safety." This is the block hide feature (CTRL-K-H) which turns the highlighting on and off. When the highlighting is off, the block cannot be moved, deleted, or copied, but the block cursor functions still work.

This feature is very useful when you want to define a small block of something to be used over and over, like a predicate name. Tricks like this can save you thousands upon thousands of characters of typing.

Block copy and block move are the same operation, except that the latter will delete the block from its original position in your text file. They are both begun in the same way. After the block of text is marked, move the cursor to the new position for that chunk of text. CTRL-K-V will move the marked block almost instantly to this new place, removing it from the old location and closing up the lines of text to reflect this. CTRL-K-C simply makes an exact copy of the block, but leave it intact at the old location. Both are useful, powerful, and fast commands.

The Main Menu

As we've already seen, hitting the F1 function key (usually on the far left of your keyboard), causes a "main menu" to pop up, its position depending on where your cursor is located in the editor window. This is not to be confused with the main menu bar, it is merely a vertical submenu. The first choice on this submenu is "Help information." That selection will be already highlighted when the menu appears, so just punch your Return key to activate.

The PROLOG.HLP file appears in an auxiliary window, as we've already discussed. Again, CTRL-F10 will expand this to a full screen view and the various cursor key commands will let you move about in the file to refresh your memory on some function or other, such as the screen control predicates shown in Fig. 6-8. Also, remember that you can edit the PROLOG.HLP file just like you would a program file, adding in your own notes and other helpful information that you might need quick access to.

The second selection on the Main Menu submenu is "Block Functions." These are redundant to the key command combinations and the function keys. Some of these block functions, and the other types described below, have *three* methods of activation. The block commands on the main menu serve as a sort of on-line help. Hit F1 to bring up the menu, select Blocks Functions, then choose the one you want and it will be executed.

The block functions that may be accessed in this manner are Search

```
──────────────────────────── Help ────────────────────────────
SCREEN HANDLING
===============
attribute(Attr)
        (integer) -- (inp) (outp)

cursor(Row,Column)
        (integer,integer) -- (inp,inp) (outp,outp)

cursorform(Startline,Endline)    0<Startline<14, 0<Endline<14
        (integer,integer) -- (inp,inp)

field_str(Row,Column,Length,String)
        (integer,integer,integer,string) -- (inp,inp,inp,inp) (inp,inp,inp,out

field_attr(Row,Column,Length,Attr)
        (integer,integer,integer,integer)
        -- (inp,inp,inp,inp) (inp,inp,inp,outp)

scr_char(Row,Column,Char)
        (integer,integer,char) -- (inp,inp,inp) (inp,inp,outp)

scr_attr(Row,Column,Attr)
```

Fig. 6-8. Various predicate forms, such as these for screen control, are available via a help window while you are editing.

Text, Search Again, Replace Text, Replace Again, Copy Text, Copy Again, Move Block, Move Again, Remove Block, and Main Menu which returns you to the submenu titled that, *not* the main menu bar.

One handy feature of the Blocks Function submenu and the next three submenus is that they will come back up when the F1 key is hit *without* having to go through the Main Menu submenu. They will continue to do so until you choose Main Menu as a selection. Thus, if you are doing a series of block functions, this can be extremely convenient.

The next selection on the Main Menu submenu is Positions. These refer to cursor functions. The selections here reflect the cursor control operations herein discussed. The selections are Start Text (which moves the cursor up to the beginning of text), End Text, Start Line, End Line, Page Up, Page Down, Word Left, Word Right, Go To Line (move the cursor to a specific line number), Current Line (make the line the cursor is now residing on the current line), and Main Menu, which resets to the misnamed submenu brought up by the F1 key in the editor window.

Delete Keys is the next selection. These are redundancies of the delete functions. The selections are Delete Line (the entire line that the cursor is currently on), Delete To End Of Line (from where the cursor now is), Delete Character (the one the cursor is on), Delete Character To Left (leaving intact the one on which the cursor rests), and Main Menu to reset.

The Status selection is redundant in a different way. It confirms what you can also determine from the status line appearing on top of the editor window. Additionally it allows you to reset these options. Since you have the option of expanding the editor window to cover that line, perhaps this selection is not so redundant, after all. The selections are Auto Indent On/Off, Insert/Overwrite, and Main Menu.

The selections External Copy and Aux Edit on the Main Menu submenu bring up the file-loading windows, just as Load does on the Files selection from the main menu bar. The difference is that the file chosen is loaded into the auxiliary edit window either for block transfer to your current program or to be edited on its own.

The last selection is Quit Edit, which like the Esc key or the F10 key, will take you out of the edit window deposit you back on the main menu bar.

Reading Blocks from Disk

Finally in our block party, we come to another big timesaver, reading a block from disk (Fig. 6-9). This one is handy because you could develop a library of standard routines, loading them in by blocks as you put your programs together.

To get a block from the disk, move the cursor to the point in your program where you want to insert the block. Then hit the F9 function key or the command CTRL-K-R. The Load option of the Files submenu will pop up, as will the auxiliary editor window and the Files submenu.

You can either enter the name of the file that contains the subprogram, or of any other block that you want to enter into your current program. If you do not remember the name, hit the Return key and a directory window pops up. Use the arrow keys to highlight the file name you need, then hit Return.

```
      Run       Compile      Edit      Options      Files      Setup      Quit

 Editor                                            |Load                  |g
| Line 1       Col 1      Indent   Inser
|/* Program 1 */                     |File name:
|/*
|   Enter the goal on page 18 of the manual.      |Copy
|   Some valuable notes are at the bottom         |Rename
|   of this program.                              |File Name
|*/                      |External copy  Line 1   |Module list          |t   Insert
|                        |                        |Zap file in editor
|domains                 |                        |Erase
|    person, activity = s|                        |Operating system
|                        |
|predicates              |
|    likes(person,activit|
|                        |
|clauses                 |
|    likes(ellen,tennis).|
|    likes(john,football)|
|    likes(tom,baseball).|
|    likes(eric,swimming)
Use first letter of option  or  select with  ->  or  <-
```

Fig. 6-9. You may copy portions of other files into the program currently in the editor window.

The file will appear in the Auxiliary Editor window, which pops up to overlay the four windows of the environment already on the screen. Now find and highlight the block you want to move. Unlike in the main editor window, the sequence here is important: designate the start first and the end last. As soon as you press CTRL-K-K to end the block, it will be immediately transferred to the editor window at the place where you left the cursor, and the auxiliary editor window will disappear.

This may also be done in reverse, writing a block from the file being currently edited to disk. This is accomplished with the CTRL-K-W command combination.

SEARCH AND REPLACE

The Turbo Prolog editor has several commands built into it that facilitate your finding and, optionally, replacing strings of text. A string is any group of text and/or numbers. The predicate

```
likes (ralph,prolog) if language (turbo_prolog)
```

is a string.

When you have a two- or three- or four-hundred-line program, finding one occurrence of a particular predicate could become time-consuming. The search commands make it incredibly easy. Type either CTRL-Q-F or hit the F3 function key. You will be asked for the string you want to find. It is not necessary to enter the whole string, only enough of it to be unique. In fact, you are limited to strings of 25 characters or less, both in searching and in replacing automatically.

Once the string to be searched for is entered, you must tell Turbo Prolog so it can begin execution. If you started with CTRL-Q-F, hit Return; if you used the F3 key finish the operation by hitting it again. Once the string is found, you can find the next occurrence of it with the command combinations CTRL-L or Shift-F3.

The second version of the search command finds and automatically replaces the search string. You are again limited to strings of 25 characters or less. The operation is begun by CTRL-Q-A or the F4 function key. When you enter this command you are prompted for the search string. Type it in. If you used F4, hit F4 again. If you use the control key combination, press the Return key.

You will be asked if you want a global or local find and replace. If you pick local, only the first occurrence of the text string will be found and replaced. If global is chosen then all occurrences of the string from the current cursor position to the end of the file will be searched out and optionally replaced.

You will be asked one more question: do you want to be prompted before a replacement is carried out? If you answer **no**, the finding and replacing is done automatically. If you answer **yes**, then each time the string is found you will be queried **Replace (Y/N)**. Thus, you can selectively search and replace. In this case, shift-F4 or CTRL-L repeats the latest find and replace operation exactly as if all information had been re-entered.

The Esc key, as in other operations, may be used to abort and escape from this command at any time.

AUTO INDENT

The cursor doesn't always return all the way to the left side of your screen when Return is hit. In fact, if Auto Indent is turned on, it will only return to the left as far as the starting column of the previous line. This feature is included so that your program files will be better organized and easier to read (Fig. 6-10).

If you need to change the column the cursor returns to, you may use the left or right arrow keys or the Tab key. The unshifted tab key jumps you right and, shifted, will jump you left. I recommend that you use this method to obtain your indents, thus making them all standard. The indentation is set for 8 spaces each time the Tab key is hit. Twice would mean 16 spaces from the left margin, and so on. CTRL-I is the equivalent.

You may turn the auto indent off and on by using the key combination CTRL-Q-I. This works as a toggle switch. On the line directly above the editor window, the word **indent** will be present to indicate when auto indent is on.

```
    Run     Compile     Edit     Options     Files     Setup     Quit

---------------------- Editor ----------------    -------- Dialog --------
 Line 1      Col 1      Indent  Insert  EXAMPL01.
 ------------------------------
        Editor status
 ------------------------------of the manual.
 Ctrl QI: Auto indent on/off   the bottom
 Ins    : Insert/Overwrite
          Main menu
 ------------------------------
domains
     person, activity = symbol

predicates
     likes(person,activity)

clauses                                            -------- Trace --------
     likes(ellen,tennis).
     likes(john,football).
     likes(tom,baseball).
     likes(eric,swimming).

F1:Help F3:Search F4:Subst F5:Copy F6:Move F7:Del F8:ExtEdit F9:ExtCopy F10:End
```

Fig. 6-10. This pop-down menu shows the insert and auto-indent status of the editor.

FUNCTION KEYS

The functions keys are labeled F1 - F10, and are defined by the software in control of your computer. In the case of Turbo Prolog, all ten keys perform specific commands related to the built-in editor (refer back to Fig 6-7).

Nonstandard keyboards may not have function keys, and you will have to find an equivalent method of performing the command. Turbo Prolog lends itself to compromises by providing methods of redefining key functions.

When you are using the program editor, on-screen help is available to help you remember these function assignments: just hit the F1 key.

Three of the other nine function keys, also defined, have a dual function when used in combination with the shift key.

The F2 key is a handy way to get about in a large program. The Turbo Prolog editor numbers lines sequentially from top to bottom—the line number you are currently on is indicated on the line just above the editor window, along with the column number and other information, such as whether auto indent is on, whether the insert or overwrite mode is active, and the name of the file currently being edited.

The F2 key will let you go to a specific line almost instantaneously. Merely hit the F2 key once. You will be asked what line number to move to. Enter the number and hit F2 again and the cursor moves to that line.

The F3 key is used for search and replace. Shift-F3 is used to repeat the search command for the same string.

F4 is the same as CTRL-Q-A, the replace function; shift-F4 tells the editor to replace the next occurrence of the string with that in the one just completed.

The F5 key is the same as the block copy command CTRL-K-C. Shift-F5 repeats the function.

F6 is the same as block move, F7 the same as block delete. F8 causes the auxiliary editor window to pop up and F9 is used to copy a block from an external program or subroutine file on disk. Shift-F9, in Version 1.1 of Turbo Prolog and higher, uncovers the other windows of the programming environment. You can rotate through them and resize whichever you stop on with the arrow keys. Hitting Return ends this process.

The F10 key, like Esc, causes you to exit the editor window and deposits you back on the main menu bar. The CTRL-F10 key combination works not only in the editor window but in the others, as well. Hitting this command sequence causes the current window to occupy the entire screen. Hitting the command again returns the current window to its original size.

Chapter 7

Objects and Relationships

PROLOG WAS DEVELOPED TO SOLVE LOGIC PROBLEMS IN AN ORDERly progression by the use of backward reasoning or *backtracking.* Because of this structure, the language Prolog, in its various implementations, is very good for artificial intelligence applications. The two most important of these being natural language recognition and expert systems.

Such applications are made possible by Prolog's ability to take the elements of logic programming and "infer" or reason out a conclusion based on stated conditions. Turbo Prolog, specifically, has the ability built-in to create databases and to compare the facts in it with its "inference engine." This latter is the part that lets you write software which *finds its own path* to the answer.

The basic building blocks of Prolog are relationships, specifically relationships of objects to one another. An object is anything that can be represented symbolically in your programs. Some examples could be potato, banana, and love.

All of these, even proper names, start with lowercase letters. Starting a word with an uppercase letter means that it is a variable instead of an object.

There is a wide range of difference between the objects listed above. One of them, love, is not even a tangible thing. For Turbo prolog to use inference via backwards reasoning to obtain logical answers in regards to your queries, it must know the *relationships* these objects have (Fig. 7-1). So you define these in your program. A potato is vegetable, banana is fruit, love is an emotion and so on. Other relationships can be specified as well, such as persons eat vegetables, meat, fruit, cats eat meat, persons love cats, etc.

Knowing these relationships, a Prolog program would then be able to answer questions about the relationships. Adding to the objects and relationships dramatically increases the power of the program.

To actually tell Turbo Prolog the objects and their relationships is a simple process. Using the editor window in the programming environment, type them in. The only thing even semi-involved about this is to use the proper *syntax.*

Syntax means that the objects and relationships must be in a format recognizable to the compiler as being the definition of an object/relationship. In Turbo Prolog this takes the form relationship (object), as in **meat(steak)** or **animal(cat).**

When we use the format *relationship(object)*, the relationship is known as the *predicate* and the object is referred to as the *argument.*

We might define the predicate **eats(food)**. Then, down in the clauses sections we could list the specific facts and the program would recognize the relationships. The facts might be **eats(potato)**, **eats(beans)**, **eats(peas)**, and **eats(spinach)**. Expanding with more relationships, we can further define that the foods referred to are all vegetables: **vegetable(potato)**, **vegetable(beans)**, **vegetable(peas)**, and **vegetable(spinach)**.

```
domains

        vegetable, food = symbol

predicates

        vegetable(food)
        eats(vegetable)

clauses

        eats(potato).
        eats(beans).
        eats(peas).
        eats(spinach).
        vegetable(potato).
        vegetable(beans).
        vegetable(peas).
        vegetable(spinach).
```

Fig. 7-1. This Turbo Prolog program shows how objects and relationships are entered.

When we run the program the dialog window is raised and we could ask **eats(What)**; an uppercase letter denotes a variable. Prolog checks its facts, determines that one eats food, then proceeds to see what this might be. An answer is found: potato is food. The program then backtracks to see if any other solutions exist. Three others are found. In the dialog window appears the answer: **What = potato, What = beans, What = peas, What = spinach, 4 solutions.**

PROGRAM STRUCTURE

A Turbo Prolog program is a text file that the system compiles into a series of machine language commands that your computer can understand and act on. Because these programs are nothing but text files, you are as much a word processor as a programmer.

Turbo Prolog can only understand the rules and facts you have entered if they are in the proper format, or syntax. If you use the wrong syntax—misnamed, misspelled, or whatever—the programming environment will put an error message at the bottom of the screen and point to the place in the text where the mistake is.

There are several parts to a Turbo Prolog program; not all have to be present in every program. *Comments* resemble the REM (remarks) statement in BASIC; a programmer can put notes into the program that are not changed into machine language and executed. Any text preceded by a slash-asterisk (>/*) and ended with an asterisk-slash (*/) will be interpreted as a comment no matter how many lines it takes up. You can use normal capitalization within the commentary bounds, and you may have as many comments per program as are necessary. Comments may be inserted anywhere in the program.

Following the initial comments, most Turbo Prolog programs will be divided into four main divisions—*domains, predicates, goals,* and *clauses.* A fifth category—*databases*—will be discussed in a later chapter.

The domains section is indicated simply by the word "domains" flush against the left margin. Here variables are declared.

Turbo prolog first wants to know about the types of arguments your predicates will be using, called *type checking.* Here is the major place where Borland departed from the more "standard" Clocksin and Mellish Prologs.

The reason for what AI hackers consider such a disgusting departure from the pure beauty of logic programming actually has two practical reasons behind it. The first is obviously commercial. If Turbo Prolog resembles the company's fantastically successful Turbo Pascal, then sales can only increase. The other is perhaps more reasonable to the end user (that's us). Turbo Prolog is designed to work in the limited memory environment of the IBM PC and compatibles rather than the wider playing field of mainframe computers or the DEC VAXes used in the AI fastnesses of academia. If Turbo Prolog knows what type of variables it's working with, compilation and other memory management can be more efficiently used.

The second section of a Turbo Prolog program contains the *predicates* definitions, and begins where the word predicates is found flush against the left margin. Predicates define the relationships. An example would be **person(name)**, where name is a symbol domain. This predicate describes a series of clauses or rules found in the clauses section. If you wish to use a predicate other than one of the built-in predicates in the clauses or goal sections, it must first be formally declared here.

The *clauses* section begins following the word "clauses" found flush against the left margin. Clauses are the rules and relationship defined by the predicates and made up of various domains. In using clauses the simple predicate **person(name)** could define the clauses **person(monica)**, **person(heather)**, **person(kimberly)**, **person(susie)**. Since these names are symbols rather than variables, they all must begin with lowercase letters.

You may also specify an internal goal in the goal section, following the word goal located against the left margin. If this section is missing, the dialog window will appear and you can type in goals manually. For external goals it is assumed that you want to see the results; they are automatically displayed on the screen. The way internal goals display results, however, must be specified. The goal is satisfied only once unless you tell the program to backtrack and give you all possible solutions.

Instructions to display the goals are simple. In our example, we would add two lines: **person(Who)** and **write(Who)**. The first examines the clauses to try to prove or disprove the goal, and the write predicate (a predefined one that may always be used without definition) will write the answer in the **Who** variable, which must begin.

To get the program to backtrack and give us the rest of the solutions, add two more predefined predicates in your goal section. Because they are predefined, no declaration is necessary. First, behind **write(Who)**, add **nl**, (making sure the commas are included as shown and the period that was there is removed). This is merely a line return to prevent the answers from jumbling up on one line. Now, directly below, put **fail.**, making sure it ends with a period.

The **fail** predicate will cause the program to backtrack and find all solutions (Fig. 7-2), ending only when it fails to find another. Running the program now automatically responds with the results we now know it should—**monica**, **heather**, **kimberly**, and **susie**. Again, I encourage you to experiment with "playtime" programs like this, constantly elaborating the logic. This also will speed up the learning process.

A PROGRAM

Let's do a little programming. Bring up the programming environment: two drive systems put the Turbo Prolog Program Disk into drive A: and, at the A> prompt, type **PROLOG** (upper- or lowercase or any mixture of them is okay). The Turbo Prolog title screen will appear. Hard disk users have to change to the proper directory, usually be on drive C:. Then type the word **PROLOG** and the title screen will appear.

Make sure the directory paths and the name of the work file are set as you need them to be. If not, hit the space bar anyway (as it tells you to on the bottom of the screen), only instead of going from the main menu bar to the editor window to start a program, first to access the Setup pull down submenu and make whatever changes are needed.

Once the programming environment is set up to your liking, you are ready to create a program. In this case the working file is almost certainly **WORK.PRO**, indicated on the initial title screen and also on the first line of the editor window on the programming environment screen (Fig. 7-3). Once a program is entered, you can always save it under another name if you prefer.

Enter the editor window by selecting Edit on the main menu bar, by typing an **E** (upper- or lowercase), or using the arrow keys to cause Edit to be highlighted, then hitting the Return key. You are ready to start entering your Turbo prolog program.

I suggest you always title your program using the comments feature, and maybe a short note to the user explaining what the program does and any special considerations. You can easily modify this comment area during the course of your program, but get it started now to remind you to do so. Good comments (Fig. 7-4) are one of the most important parts of programming in any language.

```
domains
        name = symbol
predicates
        person(name)
goal
        person(Who),
        write(Who),nl,
        fail.

clauses
        person(monica).
        person(heather).
        person(kimberly).
        person(susie).
```

Fig. 7-2. Adding a fail predicate will cause a Turbo Prolog program to backtrack until it finds all the solutions it can based on the information it knows. Fail is one of several ways you can control Turbo Prolog's search for solutions.

```
 Run     Compile     Edit     Options     Files     Setup     Quit

-------------------- Editor --------------------  ------------ Dialog ------------
 Line 1      Col 1      Indent   Insert   WORK.PRO





-------------------- Message -------------------  ------------ Trace -------------



Use first letter of option  or  select with  ->  or  <-
```

Fig. 7-3. The starting layout of the Turbo Prolog programming environment.

Each line you type should be terminated by a carriage return. If you make a mistake, simply use the arrow keys to move the cursor to the mistake and use the Del or backspace keys to remove the error and type in the correction.

During the rest of this chapter, to demonstrate relationships, Figs. 7-5 through 7-8 show the development of a whimsical program entitled "What Does The President Eat?" Don't worry if you don't understand all the concepts immediately; they will be explained in later chapters, and you can refer back. Start the program by entering the title and any comments you wish.

```
/*______________________________________________________________________*/
/*(*)(*)(*)(*)(*)(*)(*)(*)(*)(*)(*)(*)(*)(*)(*)(*)(*)(*)(*)(*)(*)(*)*/
/*""""""""""""""""""""""""""""""""""""""""""""""""""""""""""""""""""""*/
/*                                                                    */
/*    __        __                                                    */
/*    l_)       l_)                                                   */
/*    l\alph_   l\oberts_     Artificial Intelligence Baked To Order  */
/*    \______)   \______)                                             */
/*--------------------------------------------------------------------*/
/* 10/27/86        Program #34 -- taking a list of leftovers          */
/*                 in the refrigerator and giving you recipes.        */
/*______________________________________________________________________*/
/*(*)(*)(*)(*)(*)(*)(*)(*)(*)(*)(*)(*)(*)(*)(*)(*)(*)(*)(*)(*)(*)(*)*/
/*""""""""""""""""""""""""""""""""""""""""""""""""""""""""""""""""""""*/
```

Fig. 7-4. Using the comment symbols and a little imagination lets you create spiffy headers for your Turbo Prolog programs.

```
/*  W H A T   D O E S   T H E   P R E S I D E N T   E A T ?

    A somewhat whimiscal Turbo Prolog demonstration program
       written especially for this book by Ralph Roberts

                          (version 1)

    (note that these top lines are just a single comment)    */

domains
        thing = symbol

predicates
        vegetable (thing)
        meat (thing)
        animal (thing)
        person (thing)
        car (thing)

clauses
        vegetable (potato).
        vegetable (beans).
        vegetable (peas).
        vegetable (spinach).
        meat (steak).
        meat (fish).
        meat (pork).
        animal (cat).
        person (ronald_reagan).
        car (volvo).
        car (ford).
```

Fig. 7-5. The start of our whimsical demo program. Note that it is made up only of objects and relationships.

Hit Return a couple of times just to put some space between the start of your program and the comments. This enhances readability. You should be on Column 1 (the status line at the top of the editor window tells you) and on Line 3, 4, 5, or whatever. Type the word **domains** in lowercase. Hit Return twice. Type the word **predicates**. Hit Return two more times. Type the word **clauses**. Hit Return just once.

We'll enter some objects and relationships which we'll develop into a more powerful program later by adding rules. Your cursor should be at the beginning of the line immediately below the word clauses.

Entering the clauses before doing the top of the program, may seem unusual to you at first, but it is easier. As you will soon see, determining what objects you need in the logical structure of your program will make

```
    /* W H A T   D O E S   T H E   P R E S I D E N T   E A T ?

       A somewhat whimiscal Turbo Prolog demonstration program
          written especially for this book by Ralph Roberts

                             (version 3)

      (note that these top lines are just a single comment)    */

domains
        thing = symbol

predicates
        vegetable (thing)
        meat (thing)
        animal (thing)
        person (thing)
        car (thing)
        eats (thing)             /* add an "eats" predicate */
clauses
        eats(X):-                /* add a rule for eating */
                vegetable(X) or meat(X).
        vegetable (potato).
        vegetable (beans).
        vegetable (peas).
        vegetable (spinach).
        meat (steak).
        meat (fish).
        meat (pork).
        animal (cat).
        person (ronald_reagan).
        car (volvo).
        car (ford).

goal
        person(ronald_reagan),
        eats(Food),
        write(Food),nl,
        fail.
```

Fig. 7-6. Adding a goal section causes the program to automatically find out what the President eats . . . at least from the facts available to it.

entering the predicates and domains much simpler.

Hit the Tab key to move the cursor left eight spaces to indent the list of clauses we are about to enter.

You must use all lowercase; each clause must end with a period so

```
   /*  W H A T   D O E S   T H E   P R E S I D E N T   E A T ?

     A somewhat whimiscal Turbo Prolog demonstration program
        written especially for this book by Ralph Roberts

                            (version 2)

      (note that these top lines are just a single comment)    */

domains
        thing = symbol

predicates
        vegetable (thing)
        meat (thing)
        animal (thing)
        person (thing)
        car (thing)
        eats (thing)              /* add an "eats" predicate */
clauses
        eats(X):-                 /* add a rule for eating */
                vegetable(X) or meat(X).
        vegetable (potato).
        vegetable (beans).
        vegetable (peas).
        vegetable (spinach).
        meat (steak).
        meat (fish).
        meat (pork).
        animal (cat).
        person (ronald_reagan).
        car (volvo).
        car (ford).
```

Fig. 7-7. Now we add a rule to our program.

the compiler can recognize that each fact is fully defined. End each line by hitting Return. If you have auto indent turned on, the cursor will move down directly under the first letter of the preceding clause. If not, you can space in by using the Tab key, or by hitting the space bar eight times. Auto indent may be toggled on by the commands CTRL-V or by pressing the insert (Ins) key.

Enter the following clauses, one above the other:

```
vegetable(potato).
 vegetable(beans).
```

```
   /* W H A T   D O E S   T H E   P R E S I D E N T   E A T ?

      A somewhat whimiscal Turbo Prolog demonstration program
         written especially for this book by Ralph Roberts
                              (version 4)      */
domains
        thing = symbol
predicates
        vegetable (thing)
        meat (thing)
        fruit (thing)
        animal (thing)
        person (thing)
        car (thing)
        eats (thing)
        veggiewrite
        meatwrite
        fruitwrite
clauses
        eats(X):-               /* add a rule for eating */
                vegetable(X) and veggiewrite
                or meat(X) and meatwrite
                or fruit(X) and fruitwrite.
        veggiewrite:-gotowindow(2). /* conditional branching */
        meatwrite:-  gotowindow(3). /* to the appropriate window */
        fruitwrite:- gotowindow(4).
        vegetable (potato).
        vegetable (beans).
        vegetable (peas).
        vegetable (spinach).
        meat (steak).
        meat (fish).
        meat (pork).
        meat (barbeque).
        meat (spareribs).
        meat (shrimp).
        fruit (apple).
        fruit (banana).
        fruit (orange).
        fruit (grapefruit).
        fruit (plum).
        animal (cat).
        person (ronald_reagan).
        car (volvo).
        car (ford).
goal
        clearwindow,
        makewindow(1,7,15,"What Does The President Eat?",0,0,25,80),
        makewindow(2,7,15,"Vegetables",10,10,10,15),
```

```
makewindow(3,7,15,"Meats",10,30,10,15),
makewindow(4,7,15,"Fruits",10,50,10,15),
person(ronald_reagan),
eats(Food),
write(Food),nl,
gotowindow(1),
fail.
```

Fig. 7-8. Finally we add more possible foods, plus some windowing predicates to "pretty print" the information to the screen. There are few limits to the level of elaboration you can achieve in a Turbo Prolog program.

```
vegetable(peas).
vegetable(spinach).
meat(steak).
meat(fish).
meat(pork).
animal(cat).
person(ronald__reagan).
car(volvo).
car(ford).
```

Note that ronald__reagan is joined by an underline character. In using more than one word as a Prolog object, it must be combined with an underline or the compiler will try to interpret it as two words, or it must be defined by quotation marks:

```
person("Ronald Reagan").
```

Now use the arrow keys to move your cursor up the screen to the line directly below the word predicates. Again use the Tab key, setting up the same indent used under clauses.

The predicates section of a Turbo Prolog program defines the relationships expressed in the clauses section. For now we'll just call them all things. So, one above the other (but leave off the period this time) enter:

```
vegetable(thing)
meat(thing)
animal(thing)
person(thing)
car(thing)
```

Turbo prolog wants to know what *kind* of things these are. Use the arrow keys to move the cursor to the first position on the line under domains. Hit the Tab key, and enter thing = symbol. A symbol is just a name, and must always start with a lowercase letter. Since all our objects are currently defined as things, only the one domain declaration is necessary.

Save the program to a file. When you are asked for the name of the file, just the number 7, which will cause this version of our program to be saved as 7.PRO. on your disk. Turbo Prolog puts the .PRO extension on automatically. Now tap the Esc key until you are back to the main menu bar; a couple of times should do it.

COMPILING AND RUNNING

We now have a text file in a format that Turbo Prolog can recognize as a program. Compiling the program turns it into machine language instructions which your computer can use.

Typing **R** on the main menu bar, or selecting the Run option with the arrow keys and hitting Return, will cause what you've typed in to be compiled in your computer's working memory. Think of this as a trial run. If the program works as you envisioned it doing, then the Options submenu can be accessed, .EXE selected, and (moving back to the main menu bar and pickingCompile, a stand-alone executable program can be created. But first, just run what you have and see if it works.

Turbo Prolog's built-in syntax checker will give you an error message in the message window, and the cursor will appear in the editor window at the place where the error exists. You may then correct the error and press the F10 function key to try compiling again. If you have typed the program in correctly this will be indicated by activation of the dialog window; the word **Goal**: will be displayed and the cursor will pause just to the right of it.

Our program has a number of relationships defined, but no rules concerning what it should do with them. Still, you can experiment in the dialog window. Try typing in **vegetable(What)**. Note that the variable enclosed in the parentheses starts with an uppercase letter. You may have longer, more descriptive variable names, just as long as the first letter is uppercase and spaces are replaced by the underline character:

```
Vegetables_served_on_the_White_House_table
```

is a perfectly legitimate if somewhat unwieldy variable name.

Entering **vegetable(What)** gives this program something it knows how to handle. You will immediately get the answers **What = potato, What = beans, What = peas,** and **What = spinach.**

Ask it **person(Who)** and you get **ronald_reagan**. Play with the program for awhile and see what else you can find out. You may halt the program and exit the dialog window by pressing the Esc key. This returns you to the main menu bar.

EVALUATING RELATIONSHIPS

Turbo Prolog evaluates clauses in an orderly fashion from top to bottom and from left to right. Objects can have a number of relationships of varying complexity. Such diversity as this:

```
vegetable(potato)
 idaho(potato)
 maine(potato)
 peeled(potato)
 sweet(potato)
 hot(potato)
 small(potato)
 boiled(potato)
```

are all legitimate relationships of the **potato** object and all may exist simultaneously!

A relation can involve one, two, three, or more objects. The car object might be expanded to:

```
car(volvo), green, station_wagon, 1975)
```

and

```
car(ford, black, special_secret_service_sedan, 1985)
```

Just remember that the predicate must be declared to reflect these clauses. In this case that might be:

```
car(brand, color, type, model_year)
```

Clauses, that belong to the same predicate must be grouped together in your program declarations. Thus, all car clauses would be listed one over the other in the clauses section.

VARIABLES

In the program examples above we have used *variables* such as **Who**, **What**, and **Brand**. Variable names in Turbo Prolog must begin with a capital letter, after which any combination of upper- or lowercase letters, numbers, and underline characters may be used. Such names as those:

```
An_entirely_correctly_named_variable
Sales_10_29_86
```

```
Blue_Fords
Green_Volvos
Blond_Ladies
Marvin
```

are all perfectly acceptable. Use variable names that help you keep track of program logic. (Humor is acceptable, but be sure to *comment* everything properly.

Except for the first character of the variable name, Turbo Prolog does not care how you mix upper- and lowercase letters, so variables may also be named as ExpenseAccount, YellowSweaters, RedApples, and BooksAboutTurboProlog. Doing this will help you to make them more readable.

You may also use *blank* variables. Take this predicate, for example:

```
owns(person, color house)
```

We might just want to know if anyone has a red house. Entering the goal owns(_, red,_) in the dialog window would give us a True if someone has a red house. Or, entering owns(_, Color, _) would give a list of the different colored house in the database, as in Color=red, Color=white, Color=purple, etc. Blank variables can be very handy, simplifying your database queries.

When a goal argument is a variable, such as in vegetable (What), Turbo Prolog handles it very specially during the compilation process. It will examine each clause and instantiate the variable to the value in the clause. That is, it temporarily makes the variable equal to the corresponding one in the particular clause being examined. In Turbo Prolog parlance this is called *binding*. A *bound variable* is one with a specific value, while a free variable can be instantiated at will by the program.

If the instantiated variable satisfies the argument, this is reported to you in the dialog window with the variable still equal to the value in the clause. Turbo Prolog then examines the next clause, resetting the variable value to equal it and seeing if this one agrees with its argument.

Thus it finds all clauses that answer the question, and gives you perhaps several answers to that question, all correct. These, as we will see in the next chapter, may be further refined by applying rules to limit the number of answers you get.

Chapter 8

Declarations, Clauses, Rules and More

THE ORDINARY OBJECTS AND RELATIONSHIPS WE DISCUSSED IN the last chapter are just a taste of what Turbo Prolog provides for you—mere appetizer to rules, multiple arguments, compound goals, tracing, and the incredible power of logical backtracking. The nice thing about all this is that while Turbo Prolog is extremely powerful, these basic building blocks of logic programming are simple and easy to learn and use. Objects and relationships were a snap, right? So is the rest of it.

First, we must learn some rules of the road, meaning the way we conduct ourselves—like not passing on the right on a two-lane road, especially if there's a guard rail or you are on a bridge. In other words, how to enter and use various parts of Turbo Prolog's language and environment (Fig. 8-1 and Fig. 8-2).

Names (also called *terms*) are a very important part of Turbo Prolog programs. They designate symbolic constants, domains, predicates, and variables. The syntax for the name is a letter or underline character followed by any combination of letters, numbers, and underline characters. There are two very important restrictions on this.

First, names of symbolic constants must start with a lowercase letter. What are symbolic constants? In the program we're working on, we said that thing was a symbol in our domains declaration. Right now we are calling such items as potatoes, steaks, fords, and ronald_reagans things. This will be refined shortly, but essentially this is what a symbolic constant is—an object and relationship that Turbo Prolog can recog-

```
        Run      Compile      Edit      Options      Files      Setup      Quit

                                       Editor  |Load            |
 Line 1      Col 1      Indent   Inser
/* Answer to exercise on Page 8 */     |File name:                          |
/*
  This is the fi           Directory: B:çANSWERSç*.PRO
  it has been ch| ANS08.PRO       ANS135.PRO      ANS141.PRO      ANS142.PRO
  works the same| ANS143.PRO      ANS146.PRO      ANS147.PRO      ANS20.PRO
  & WRITEF. The | ANS24.PRO       ANS29.PRO       ANS30.PRO       ANS37.PRO
  starts a comme| ANS42-A.PRO     ANS42-B.PRO     ANS44.PRO       ANS45-A.PRO
  ends a comment| ANS45-B.PRO     ANS47.PRO       ANS48.PRO       ANS50.PRO
  start with cap| ANS58.PRO       ANS61-A.PRO     ANS61-B.PRO     ANS68.PRO
*/              | ANS69-A.PRO     ANS69-B.PRO     ANS71.PRO       ANS73.PRO

predicates
    hello

goal
    hello.

clauses

Return:Accept name   Cursor keys:Select name   S-F10:Resize window   Esc:Abort
```

Fig. 8-1. If you're not sure of the name of the file you want to load into the editor window, a pop-down list of the current drive and directory can be summoned.

```
        Run      Compile      Edit      Options      Files      Setup      Quit

                    Editor                   |Load                |g
 Line 1      Col 1      Indent   Inser
                                      |Directory: b:                 |
                                      |File mask: *.PRO              |

                                              |Rename              |
                                              |File Name           |
                                              |Module list         |
                                              |Zap file in editor  |
                                              |Erase               |
                                              |Operating system    |

                                                         Trace

Use first letter of option  or  select with  ->  or  <-
```

Fig. 8-2. Using the ".PRO" mask means that only Turbo Prolog program names will appear in the directory window.*

nize as such and handle accordingly.

The second restriction is that a variable must start with an uppercase letter or an underline character. A variable is a name that can take on different values, whereas a symbol has just one inherent value that stays the same from the initial declaration onwards.

In our example on explaining blank variables in the last chapter, we used the predicate **owns(person, color, house)**, decided that we wanted to know if anyone has a red house. Entering the goal **owns(_, red, _)** in the dialog window would give us a **True** if someone has a red house. Or enter **owns(_, Color, _)** which would give you a list of the different colored houses in the database: **Color = red, Color = white, Color = purple,** etc.

The use of the underline character gives us a wildcard designator. You will find many uses for it. Unfortunately, while a variable may be started with an underline and be followed by letters and/or numbers, it does not act as a wildcard in this instance, only as another variable. It must be used by itself to be a wildcard.

DOMAIN DECLARATIONS

In "What Does The President Eat?" we declared only the one domain: **thing = symbol**. But there are other declarations we can make. In fact, you are familiar with four general forms for use in the domains section of your programs.

The first is **name = d**, where *name* is one of the standard domain types and "d" indicates which one. These are integer, real, char, string, and symbol. An integer is a whole number falling in the range between −32768 and 37767. A real number is a decimal number such as 2.65 or 1056 or 42.64325—anywhere in the range between 1E-307 to 1E+308.

A char domain is a variable that has just one character in it. Strings can contain combinations of characters and numbers with an upper limit of 64K on the size of strings.

A symbol is simply the name of some object starting with a lowercase letter. If **expenses** is one of the names you are going to use in your program, it would be declared in the domains section as **expenses = real**, because to enter 10.51 for gas and 5.35 for oil you must handle them as the real numbers they are. Use lowercase in the declaration, even if you plan to use it as a variable. Why? because it is a name, so **expenses** is the name of your variable **Expenses**.

Many things can be syntactically alike but semantically different. What does this mean? Let's say you are writing a program for a trucking company that hauls oranges from Florida to New York. They would be concerned with tons of oranges hauled, miles traveled, and gallons of diesel fuel burned. You might declare three variables—**TonsOf Oranges, MilesTrucked,** and **FuelBurned**. You can name them anything you like as long as the variables start with an uppercase letter or an underline character.

All three variables could be either integers or real numbers, depending on the method and accuracy with which you want to handle the figures. This is one of the ways in which domain typing really pays off. We simply declare our domains on one line (using an extension of the name = d format, remembering to start with a lowercase letter even though we will be using uppercase on these variables in the goal and clauses). Thus, we would type in:

```
tonsOfOranges, milesTraveled, gallonsOfFuel = real
```

The program now knows that tons of oranges and miles traveled are numbers representing different kinds of measurements, and will avoid mixing them by doing domain checks.

The second domain form applies to *lists.* Lists are a very important part of most artificial intelligence applications. In Turbo Prolog you may declare a list domain by using the format mylist = elementDom*. The asterisk indicates that this is a list made up of elements rather than just a single variable. ElementDom can be either a domain that you define or one of those predefined, i.e., integer, real, char, string, or symbol.

Here's an example. You could declare numberlist = integer*, which would set up a domain for lists of integers such as 1, −6, 14, 147, and −38. Your list could contain many thousands of these.

Third, we may declare domains consisting of compound objects. The general form for this is:

```
myCompDom = fl(dll, ... , dln); f2(d21, ... , d2M); fM(dN1, ... , dNk)
```

These are set up by specifying a *functor* (which is simply a name for a compound object), and the domains are the subcomponents. For example, you might set up a compound domain for owners of books by declaring owners = owns(name, book), where book is a compound object in the form book(title, author). Thus an element of this domain might be:

```
owns(bill, book(the_grapes_of_wrath, steinbeck))
```

The right side of a compound domain declaratives can define several alternatives, using a semicolon or the word or to separate them. Each must have a unique functor and the descriptions for the domains of the actual subcomponents. Expanding our owners example, we could have:

```
owners = owns (name, book); likes(name, type_of_book);
   listens(name,music_type)
```

and so forth.

The fourth and final kind of domain declaration is file domains. A program can only have one line of declarations for files, but several can be included on this line. A file domain must be declared when the end user will need to refer to actual MS-DOS files by symbolic names. These symbolic names are specified as alternatives for the file domain just as we specified alternatives in the compound domains declaration. Hence, the format for declaring two files related to business bookkeeping would be **files = sales ; salary**. The general format is:

```
file = name1; name 2; ... ; nameN
```

PREDICATE DECLARATIONS

The keyword *predicates* comes after the domains section. Here you must declare the predicates that will be used in the clauses section. Every fact or rule belongs to some predicate which specifies the name of the relation involved and the types of objects included in the relationship.

A predicate is declared by typing in its name and the domains of its arguments. The general format is:

```
predname = (domain1, domain2, ... , domainN)
```

where **predname** is the name of the predicate and domains are either the user-defined ones you stated in the "domains" section of the program, or the predefined ones supplied with Turbo Prolog, such as **write**, **makewindow**, etc.

Declaring a name without arguments for a predicate is allowable, too, so as long as you have a clause including a rule to define the predicate.

Multiple predicate declarations are also possible. You might, when manipulating lists want to declare a predicate *member* which works on both numbers and names. To do this requires declaring **member** twice, as in **member(name, namelist)** for the names and **member(number, numberlist)** to handle numbers. **Name, namelist, number**, and **number list** are domains that you have previously declared in the domains section.

It is even necessary to have the same number of arguments for each of these multiple predicate declarations. Maybe you would add a third, such as **member(professional_association)**, which has just one argument, and that not even a list.

CLAUSES

A *clause* is a fact or a rule that corresponds to one of your predicates or to one of Turbo Prolog's predefined predicates. In general form, a clause is either an *atom*, or a consists of an atom followed by a colon and hyphen and then a list of atoms separated by a comma or semicolon and terminated with a period. An atom is a relationship, usually involving objects or variables.

Several keywords and their equivalent symbols play an important part in clause structure. The keyword **if**, for example, can be used in place of the colon and hyphen symbol. The keyword **and** is interchangeable with a comma, and **or** may be used in place of the semicolon.

The World Series has just ended as I write this, which gives rise to the following example of a Turbo Prolog fact:

```
baseball_team(mets, red_sox)
```

This is a fact which is made up of a single atom (which is also a *name*), and a list of *terms*. Terms can be an object from one of the six standard domains or a list, a variable, or a compound term.

COMPOUND STRUCTURES

Compound terms and structures are simply a single object that consists of other objects (called components) and a descriptive name (the *functor*). The functor is placed just in front of the components, which are enclosed in parentheses and separated with commas. The example used in the Turbo Prolog *Owners' Handbook* makes the compound term especially clear. It consists of the functor *author* and three components:

```
author(emily, bronte, 1818)
```

This is a fact—a compound object and relationship. It would be placed in the clauses section of a program with a period terminating the line that it's on.

This compound term belongs to a user-defined domain, which must be declared in the domains section. Remember, not only the compound domain which enables the compound term must be declared, but also the domains that make it up, so three lines are necessary. The first is for the compound term itself, and is written

```
authors = author (firstname, lastname, year_of_birth)
```

Then, on the next line, Turbo Prolog must be informed that firstname and lastname are symbols domains, which is accomplished by entering **firstname, lastname = symbol**. And finally, year_of_birth fits admirably as an integer, being declared as **year_of_birth = integer**.

Lists are also compound terms.

GOALS

What we want to do with any program is obtain a result or a series of results. In Turbo Prolog, these solutions are called goals and subgoals; a goal is defined as the collection of subgoals the program attempts to satisfy.

In the little programming we've done so far, the goals have been internal—the dialog window appears on the right of the screen and we type in a goal and the program tries to find a solution for it.

You may also specify an internal goal in the "goal" section. If this section is not present the dialog window appears and you can type in goals manually. It is assumed that you want to see the results of external goals and they are automatically displayed on the screen. The way internal goals display results, however, must be specified. Also, the goal is satisfied only once *unless* you have told the program to backtrack and give you all possible solutions.

Goals, since they can have subgoals, may be compound, just like domains, predicates, and clauses. By being structured like this, they can handle multiple facts or rules, by using the "glue" words AND, OR, and NOT. Because some earlier implementations of Prolog used a comma to mean **and** and a semicolon to designate **or**, you may also use this notation in Turbo Prolog.

The second example program in the Turbo Prolog *Owner's Handbook* is concerned with the predicate

```
car(brand, mileage, age, color, price)
```

There are three clauses in the "clauses" section that match the predicate:

```
car(chrysler, 130000, 3, red, 12000)
car(ford, 90000, 4, gray, 25000)
car(datsun, 8000, 1, red, 30000)
```

Note how each clause corresponds to the predicate, and that each ends with a period on the same line, to tell Turbo Prolog that this is its end (clauses may be several lines, or compounded by using **if**, **and** and **or** or their corresponding symbols of semicolon hyphen, comma, and semicolon).

To explain the clause structure further, the predicate **car** determines the relationship of all objects belonging to it. The domains of each object are specified in the domains section. The objects **age** and **price** are integers, **mileage** is a real domain (because in a used car it could very well fall above the upper limit of an integer, and **brand** and **color** are symbols, since the name is what it represents and not a variable with shifting values.

To use a simple goal, the way the predicate is set up, is somewhat awkward. Typing this in the dialog window:

```
car(Make, Odometer, Years_on_road, Body, 25000)
```

will search the database for a car costing $25,000. Don't try to hit the Return key if your dialog window is small and the whole goal will not fit on one line; Turbo Prolog will "wrap" the line around automatically for you. In fact, hitting Return will cause an error condition, since the program will think you are finished with the entry and try to execute the goal fragment.

The goal entered correctly, Turbo Prolog finds a solution and prints out the variables for you:

```
Make = ford, Odometer = 90000, Years_on_road = 4, Body = gray
```

then adds **1 solution**. If this had been a used car lot with 158 cars, there could have been 2, 3, or 18 solutions.

By using a compound goal we can ask this same question in a more natural manner and get more information. When you have mastered natural language parsing you can write programs that will accept questions in more English-like syntax. We are more likely to ask "is there a car in the database costing less than $25000?"

Turbo Prolog will check this out logically and give us an answer. To do it, you use a compound goal. You enter the car predicate in the goal, then tack on the condition with the glue word **and**, like so:

```
car(Make, Odometer, Years_on_road, Body, Cost) and Cost <
   25000.
```

To solve the goal, the program takes each clause which matches the car predicate, then looks to see if the cost is less than $25,000. If both sides of the goal are true, it backtracks to see if any more can be found. In this case only one is found, and so you get:

```
Make = chrysler, Odometer = 130000, Years_on_road = 3,
   Body = red, Cost = 12000
```

and the program adds **1 Solution**. The subgoal here (**< Cost**) uses one of the built-in Turbo Prolog relationships, this particular one being "less than."

You can also use blank variables here to determine only one or two of the objects.

The predicate **car** involves five objects. This has to be satisfied to avoid an error, so blank variables are inserted. Also, compound goals are likely here because the potential customer might want to specify an upper range in price—let's say $27,000, like the example in the *Owner's Handbook*.

The goal would then be:

car(_, Age, _, Cost, _) and Cost < 27000

Turbo Prolog finds two that fit those criteria. The program then tells you these by printing it out in the dialog window: Age = 3, Cost = 12000, Age = 4, Cost = 25000, and 2 Solutions.

The blank or anonymous variable can be plugged in wherever any other variable is used, but it is never set to a particular value and not printed out.

Blank variables may also be used to state objects and relationships as facts in the clauses section. Entering **likes (_, ice_cream)** and **breathes(_)** are equivalent to the English statements "everybody likes ice cream" and "everybody breathes."

We used the **and** operator and the "less than" above to make up a compound goal. You can also use other logical operators such as **or**, > (less than), < > (not equal to), or **not**.

RULES

Rules (Fig. 8-3 and Fig. 8-4) are nothing more than the relationship

```
|      Run       Compile      Edit       Options       Files       Setup       Quit      |

                                        Editor ---------  ----------- Dialog -----------
|  Line 1      Col 1      Indent  Insert  EXAMPL56.P|Write a word: profunity      |
|/* Program 56 */                                    |Division: pro-funity         |
|/*                                                  |Division: profu-nity         |
|  This program attempts to divide words into        |Division: profuni-ty         |
|  syllables.                                        |                             |
|*/                                                  |Press the SPACE bar          |
|                                                    |                             |
|domains                                             |                             |
|    letter = char                                   |                             |
|    word = letter*                                  |                             |
|                                                    |                             |
|predicates                                          |                             |
|    divide(word,word,word,word)                     |                             |
|    vocal(letter)                                   |                             |
------------------------ Message ---------------------                            |
|string_word                                         |                             |
|append                                              |                             |
|append                                              |                             |
|string_word                                         |                             |

Use first letter of option  or  select with  ->  or  <-
```

Fig. 8-3. Rules play a very important part in logic programming. In this ample program included in your Turbo Prolog package, rules are used to divide words into syllables.

```
    Run      Compile      Edit      Options      Files      Setup      Quit

                              Editor
  Line 1      Col 1      Indent   Insert   EXAMPL51.PRO
/* Program 51 */
/*
  For a more complete sample expert system, see
  the program GENI.PRO on the LIBRARY DISK
*/
database
    xpositive(symbol,symbol)
    xnegative(symbol,symbol)

predicates
    run
    animal_is(symbol)
    it_is(symbol)
    positive(symbol,symbol)
    negative(symbol,symbol)
    clear_facts
    remember(symbol,symbol,symbol)
    ask(symbol,symbol)

Use first letter of option  or  select with  ->  or  <-
```

Fig. 8-4. Expert systems are based on rules.

between a fact and the subgoals embedded in it that must be satisfied for the fact to be recognized as true by Turbo Prolog. A clause such as this:

```
likes(john, X) if likes(bill, X)
```

is a rule.

Let's use a more extensive example of rules by loading in the program EXAMPL05.PRO on the Library and Sample Programs disk supplied with your Turbo Package. The program is heavily commented and is a very good tool for coming quickly to grips with the concept of rules. It is a family relationship database.

There is only one domain declaration in this program, **person = symbol**. There are nine predicate declarations, all concerning the various people making up this extended family. The first two, **male(person)** and **female(person)** are pretty obvious. The next seven predicates are ones like **father(person, person)**. In English, this can be stated, "This person has that person as his or her father." The other six states of relationships are in the same format and are mother, parent, sister, brother, uncle, and grandfather.

The first 14 clauses are in the same format as the predicates, and are facts such as we are accustomed to in Turbo Prolog. If you are looking at the program, you will note that there are line spaces in-between the groups of clauses. This is fine. Turbo Prolog doesn't mind and it makes for better visibility.

Now, we come to rules! The remaining eight clauses are rules that allow Turbo Prolog to infer the family relationships of parent, brother, sister, uncle, and grandfather from the few facts given.

The first two rules determines the parents, one for the mother and one for the father. They are:

```
parent(X, Y) if mother (X, Y)
parent (X, Y) if father (X, Y)
```

Let's take these two rules and see how Turbo Prolog uses logic to decide who's a parent and of whom. Rules are very similar to the compound goals we just met.

Should we give the program the goal **parent(marilyn, Who)**, remembering that starting a word with an uppercase letter denotes a variable, we would get two solutions: **Who = beverly** and **Who = alan**. Alan and Beverly are Marilyn's parents.

How were these obtained? Turbo Prolog starts by plugging the first of its matching facts into the variable "Who" and checking them against the two parent rules. It gets one immediate match because the first for the parent/mother rule is **mother(marilyn, beverly)**. It backtracks and tries the next mother rule, but doesn't find a match because Marilyn, has only the one mother.

The second parent rule is tried. There are four father definition clauses in EXAMPL05.PR, and the first three are tried before a match is found in the fourth. There being nothing else to try, the program leaves you with its two solutions: **Who = beverly** and **Who = alan**. Neat enough, but rules get better.

The next rule determines brothers and is stated in Turbo Prolog parlance as:

```
brother(X,Y) if male(Y) and parent(X,P) and parent(Y,P) and X<>Y.
```

You may, oi course, enter long rules on more than one line by using the "glue" words and symbols like **and**, **or**, commas, semicolons, etc. This brother rule translates as, "The brother of X is Y if Y is a male and the parent of X is P and the parent of Y is P and X and Y are not the same."

Formulating rules is merely a matter of stating the logic of the operation in Turbo Prolog syntax. The next rule is for determining sisters. It is:

```
sister(X,Y) if female(Y) and parent(X,P) and parent(Y,P) and X<>Y
```

In English this reads, "The sister of X is Y if Y is female and the parent of X is P and the parent of Y is P and X and Y are not the same."

Let's break it down some more. The sister of X is Y if Y is female; that eliminates all the males. Next, the parent of X is P and the parent of Y is P. Turbo Prolog plugs in the appropriate values and checks these using the parent rules; rules can access other rules. If Alan and the lady in the variable Y share a parent, then she is his sister. Running the program and inserting the goal **sister(alan, Who)**, you will find out that Alan has one sister, Fay.

The general form for rules is:

relation (object, ... , object) ***if*** **relation (object, ... , object)**
and **... , relation (object, ... , object).**

Chapter 9

Cut and Fail

"CUT AND FAIL" ARE TWO VERY IMPORTANT WAYS OF CONTROLling your programs.

You remember that backtracking works backward from the conclusion of a statement, reducing problems into subproblems that match the conditions given as it goes. Problems can have as many solutions as the logic of the goal posed will allow. This brings us to the reasons for two of the most important and useful of Turbo Prolog's built-in predicates—*cut* (which may also be represented as !) and *fail.*

Prolog's incessant search for solutions can sometimes be a headache; you might want to find the most likely solution and "cut out" the rest of the searching (Fig. 9-1). There are a few things you, the programmer, can do to make the search for solutions more efficient. First of all, you should write the clauses in an order that fits efficient searches. It is very important that you work out the logic of the search, making sure you have the quickest way for Turbo Prolog to deduce the answers you want.

TREES

Tree structure is an important concept in computing in general and Turbo Prolog in particular. Those of us with hard disks are already familiar with it: directories branch into subdirectories, subdirectories branch into more subdirectories. You go from the root directory and travel out branches, each getting smaller (Fig. 9-2). All have files.

```
    Run      Compile      Edit      Options      Files      Setup      Quit

------------------------------ Editor ------------------------------
  Line 1      Col 1      Indent  Insert  EXAMPL45.PRO
/* Program 45 */
/*
  This program dumps a file to your screen.
  Enter a file name, like EXAMPL44.PRO.

  To make this program deterministic, two cuts
  have been added to the print_contents
  predicate.
*/

domains
    file = input

predicates
    start
    print_contents

goal

Use first letter of option  or  select with  ->  or  <-
```

Fig. 9-1. Example program 45 that comes with your Turbo Prolog package is a good example of how cuts are used.

```
    Run      Compile      Edit      Options      Files      Setup      Quit

-------------------- Editor ------------------|Load           |g ------
  Line 1      Col 1      Indent  Inser
                                  |Directory: B:\EXAMPLES              |
                                  |                                    |

                                          |Rename               |
                                          |File Name            |
                                          |Module list          |
                                          |Zap file in editor   |
                                          |Erase                |
                                          |Operating system     |

                                              ------- Trace -------

Use first letter of option  or  select with  ->  or  <-
```

Fig. 9-2. To get all the example programs on the Turbo Prolog "Library and Sample Programs" disk, you must change the current directory to \ EXAMPLES.

Prolog makes heavy use of the tree concept in its internal quest to resolve subgoals and the goal itself. It investigates each and every branch. It begins at the main goal and goes to the first subgoal, and so on, backtracking to the next branching when the prior proves either true or false.

Now here's the rub. The program really doesn't know a particular branch is a dead end until it has scurried all the way out to the first rotten nut—the first subgoal which proves to be false. A lot of time can be wasted here, and it's up to you, the programmer, to make sure this doesn't happen.

The cut predicate built into Turbo Prolog is represented by the exclamation mark character. It acts like a one-way valve, by letting Turbo Prolog try to satisfy subgoals, but *if the goal is satisfied*, not to backtrack and continue searching.

Where you place the cut predicate is, therefore, very important in restricting the search into a manageable area.

There are two main uses of the cut. The first is when you know in advance that certain possibilities will never give rise to meaningful solutions, so it would be a waste of time to have the program check them.

Second, the logic of the program may demand the cut; if, for instance, you know there can only be one answer to a particular question.

The format for a clause rule using the cut would be in the form:

```
r1 if a and b and ! and C
```

This is the way you tell Turbo Prolog that you are satisfied with the first solution of the subgoals a and b. Thus, you would get all the solutions of c that are possible from the rules and facts in your program without backtracking into a second solution of b. Hence a and b will have one value each, while c can have multiple solutions.

FAILING

On the other hand, there are times when you want to force Turbo Prolog into additional backtracking. This is done with the fail predicate, one of those built into Turbo Prolog which may be used at any time without a prior declaration in the predicates section. Fail is essentially the opposite of cut, and useful in a number of situations (Fig. 9-3).

Let's whomp up a little demo program (Fig. 9-4) to show you one of these situations and how fail works. This program will be to find and print a series of color names on your screen—blue, red, green, yellow, and purple.

For the domains section, enter domains, hit the Return key, and then tap the Tab key to indent. Type the only domains declaration we need in this program:

```
color = symbol
```

Now set up a predicates section in the same manner. To get your cursor back to the left margin, merely touch the backspace key once to collapse the tab. We have two predicates. Enter **hue(color)**, which will be the objects denoting color, with **hue** being their common relationship. Second, enter the word **shade**.

Here is something new: we have a predicate declaration without an argument. The word **shade** is used to name a rule or rules that will appear in the clauses section.

Move on to the clauses section and enter some clauses: the colors go in first, five of them. Type in **hue(blue).**, **hue(red).**, **hue(yellow).**, **hue(purple).**, and **hue(green).**, being sure to include the period that terminates them.

Run the program right now and specify the goal **hue(Color)**. (Starting **color** with an uppercase letter turns it into a variable, which is needed to store the instantiated results.) If **hue(yellow)** proves true, as it will, then Color will temporarily be bound to the value **yellow**, and so on. The goal **hue(color)**, then, will return **Color = blue**, **Color = red**, **Color = yellow**, **Color = purple**, **Color = green**, and **5 Solutions**.

It is, however, a fact of life that most programs you will be writing will not be run in the programming environment. They will be run as stand-alone programs by end users.

Stand-alone programs cannot ask you for an external goal. It is up

```
        /* generating and writing random numbers */


domains
        number = real
        num = integer
predicates
        randomgen
        repeat
clauses
        randomgen:-
                makewindow(1,78,78,"random",0,0,25,80),
                repeat,
                random(Number),
                Num = Number * 100,
                write(Num," "),
                fail.
        repeat.
        repeat:-repeat.
```

Fig. 9-3. In this program a combination of the user-defined repeat predicate and the predefined fail predicate are used to generate and write a continuous string of random numbers.

to you as the programmer to supply goals internally in the program. This is done in the goal section, set up the same way as you did for domains, clauses, and predicates. Even though there may be many subgoals, the name of this section—unlike the others—is singular, instead of plural.

An effect of specifying internal goals is that results are not printed unless this is also specified. Printing to the display screen is accomplished by using the **write** predicate, one of those already built into Turbo Prolog.

Using internal goals and the **write** predicate to print out the results halts backtracking after the first solution is found, which is why the *fail* predicate is used. This is attached to a goal or compound clause as the last subgoal. The fail predicate presents a subgoal that Turbo Prolog cannot resolve. It fails every time. Thus, even though a true result has been returned, you've fooled the program into backtracking and looking for another one while retaining the old result, so all true results are found and written out.

What if you want to limit the search? Make judicious use of the cut predicate. The search area should be restricted to the particular neighborhood of required data.

Drop down one line under the last clause, **hue(green)**, and enter **shade:-**. That's the name of our second declared predicate, **shade**, followed by a colon and a hyphen. The colon and hyphen stands for "**if.**" It means, "The clause is true if the subclauses contained within it are all true." So, **shade** may be thought of as the name of the clause which

```
    /* program 11 (demo
     the fail predicate) */

domains
        color = symbol
predicates
        hue (color)
        shade
clauses
        hue (blue).
        hue (red).
        hue (yellow).
        hue (purple).
        hue (green).
        shade:-
                hue (Color),
                write (Color),nl,
                fail.
```

Fig. 9-4. The fail predicate in Turbo Prolog has many uses. In this program it forces backtracking so that all the color names will be written to the screen.

happens to contain three other clauses.

Drop down one line and hit the Tab key. Now your automatic indentation is set 16 spaces from the left margin. Now enter three clauses, one per line. The first is **hue(Color),**. Note now that this clause is terminated with a comma instead of a period. Why? Instead of being used as an independent clause like **hue(green), hue(color)** here is part of a clause and the comma is a glue character meaning **and**, as in, "Check this subgoal and that subgoal and the last subgoal."

Enter the next subgoal on the next line. **Write(Color), nl,**. And we now use two of Turbo Prolog's built-in predicates. The first on the line, **write(Color)**, will cause the instantiated bound contents of the variable Color to be displayed on your computer screen. The second predicate on the line, **nl**, is the new line predicate.

Now, to try the program terminate this line temporarily with a period. Hit F10 to exit the editor window and select "Run" on the main menu bar. When the dialog window pops into existence, give the program a goal of **shade** and see what happens. Got just the word **blue** didn't you? Turbo Prolog resolved the last two subgoals in the clause (interchangeable in this case with subclauses) and decided that it had done enough. No backtracking occurred.

What if we want to force it to backtrack? What if we do want all those other colors?

Go back to the end of the last line in your **shade** clause. Change the period behind **nl** to a comma. Drop down one line and type in the word **fail** and put a period behind it to end the clause. Now run the program. You will get a list of colors, one per line, followed by the word **False**. You got **false** because, due to the fail predicate, Turbo Prolog thinks it never really satisfied your goal. On reaching the fail subgoal, it was always forced to backtrack.

One final exercise in showing you how fail works: put in a goal section, either before or after the clauses section. Turbo Prolog doesn't care, so do whichever is easier for you to read and understand. Drop down a line, type in the word **shade**, and end the line with a period. That's all. Now you have an internal goal! Run the program and see what happens. Neat, huh?

You probably noticed that trash from your previous run remained in the dialog window. To get rid of this, you can use the **clearwindow** built-in predicate. Merely add **clearwindow** before shade and glue the two together with a comma. Now the window will be blanked and only your answer appears. Neatness counts.

Chapter 10

Arithmetic and Recursion

THE MATHEMATICAL PREDICATES OF TURBO PROLOG MAY BE USED as subgoals, with the success or failure of those goals used in normal logic programming, which means you can include arithmetic in your search area. You might, for example, want to find all sales of a particular product in which profits were less than ten percent. This would involve two subgoals joined by **and**. One would be to find a sale involving the specific product, the other to calculate its margin of profit. Only when both conditions were true would a result be returned.

Just as it is true in evaluating other logical statements, the order of evaluation can be important in arithmetic operations. Let's take the arithmetic predicate for an example that you might have cause to construct sometime. The expression

```
A = 1 + 6 / (11 + 3) * Z
```

is very similar to what you might expect to see in BASIC. The resulting calculation is the same.

However, Turbo Prolog allows greater latitude in logical use of whatever answer the formula may return. In an actual program, you might use our example as a clause rule. The next line could have a rule such as "C and A or B"—meaning to return **True** if C and A meet the goal or if B meets it.

Arithmetic predicates may include numbers and variables (called *oper-*

ands), *operators* (add, subtract, divide, multiply), and *parentheses*. Hexadecimal (base-16) numbers are identified by a preceding dollar sign, as in $10. The value of an expression can only be calculated if all variables are bound at the time the evaluation is called for. There are two other arithmetic functions as well: mod (use all lowercase or it will be interpreted as a variable) and div. The first is modulo division, which returns the remainder of two operands. For example, in 5/3, the remainder would be 2; mod would get this result for you. The second, div, returns the quotient of dividing two operands.

Bound variables refers to the particular value the variable has at any particular moment. Free variables are instantiated: the program assigns a value to them at a particular moment when a subgoal is being evaluated, and the variable will be bound to that value only until the program backtracks and tries another solution. Depending on use, a variable may also be bound as a constant, and thus always be the same.

Take our example again, A = 1 + 6 / (11 + 3) * Z. The variable A is going to be bound to some value after the expression is evaluated. But what about the variable Z? Logically, Z must already have some value before the expression can be evaluated; it must be bound to a value. This could be taken care of in the preceding predicate as simply as declaring:

```
Z = 4
Z = Sales - Commissions
Z = NumberOfParts / NumberSubAssemblies
```

Use whatever form the logic of your program calls for, as long as Z is bound to an integer or real number fitting the expression to be evaluated.

Evaluation of mathematical expressions takes place in the order determined by the placement of the arithmetic operators, thus setting the priority of calculation. The operators with the highest priority are evaluated first: If the expression contains subexpressions in parentheses, the subexpressions are evaluated first. If the expression has a multiplication or a division operator, these operations are carried out next, working from left to right through the expression. Finally, addition and subtraction steps are accomplished, again moving from right to left.

So, if we were to bind Z to the value 4, Turbo Prolog would evaluate A = 1 + 6 / (11 + 3) * Z like this: The value (11 + 3) is the first subexpression to be resolved, giving the result 14. Now this can be divided into 6, and the answer .428571 results. Multiplying this times Z (4) gives us 1.714285 and, finally, adding 1 returns the answer of 2.714285.

Some care must be taken to make sure the receiving variable has the proper domain type. If A happens to be an integer, it will be bound only to the value 2, chopping off the decimal component. A variable that

```
Left operand                            Right operand

24                      PLUS                 34

                    Gives

                      58

          Please press the space bar
```

Fig. 10-1. One of your example programs (no. 27) is a simple calculator with separate windows for the operands and the answers.

```
    Run     Compile     Edit     Options     Files     Setup     Quit

                    Editor                                     Dialog
 Line 1     Col 1     Indent   Insert   EXAMPL27.   Goal: likes(ellen,What).
/* Program 27 */                                    What=tennis
                                                    1 Solution
predicates                                          Goal: likes(Who,What).
    run(integer)                                    Who=ellen, What=tennis
    do_sums                                         Who=john, What=football
    set_up_windows                                  Who=tom, What=baseball
    clear_windows                                   Who=eric, What=swimming
goal                                                Who=mark, What=tennis
        set_up_windows,do_sums.                     Who=bill, What=baseball
clauses                                             6 Solutions
    set_up_windows :-                               Goal:
        makewindow(1,7,7,"",0,0,25,80),
        makewindow(1,7,7,"Left operand",2,5,5,25
        makewindow(2,7,7,"",2,35,5,10),                        Trace
        nl,write(" PLUS"),
        makewindow(2,7,7,"Right operand",2,50,5,
        makewindow(3,7,7,"Gives", 10,27,5,25),
        makewindow(4,7,7,"",17,22,5,35).

Use first letter of option or select with -> or <-
```

Fig. 10-2. This is the start of the calculator program. The Turbo Prolog programming environment does not clear out the results from previous runs unless you specifically instruct it to do so.

has been declared real in the domains section, however, will take the correct answer and be bound to it.

RELATIONAL OPERATORS

Comparison—whether between two evaluated arithmetic expressions, an expression and a constant, two constants, or any other combination—is made through the use of relational operators. These are also useful in other types of logic operations, such as in the rules **'a' < 'b'** (note the use of apostrophes to denote that this is a character instead of a symbol), **bob < jane**, and **marve < marvina**, which all return a **True** because the left side of each expression comes alphabetically before the right. Thus, in addition to numeric expressions, you can also compare single characters, strings, and symbols.

Turbo Prolog will convert the comparison **'a' < 'b'** to the equivalent arithmetic expression of **97 < 98** using the corresponding ASCII code value for each character; 97 equals a lowercase a, 98 = b, 99 = c, and so forth. After this conversion the expression is evaluated and a **True** is returned. With two string or symbol values the result depends on a character-by-character comparison of corresponding positions. The result will be the same as if you had compared each set of characters separately. Comparison of corresponding positions will continue one by one from left to right until the statement is either proved or disproved.

The following operators will work in any search or condition. The first operator is the equal sign, which means whatever is on one side of the sign is exactly the same as what is on the other side, as in **BushelsOfApples = NumberOfBaskets** or **A = B/34**.

The operator < is less than, < = means less than or equal to; > is greater than, > = denotes greater than or equal to; and < > or > < mean different from or not equal to.

MATHEMATICAL PREDICATES

There are a number of standard mathematics-related predicates built into Turbo Prolog. For predefined predicates declaration is not necessary since they already exist. Each of these predicates use the standard *relationship(object)* format. They will also perform like the arithmetic functions covered above—you can use them in expressions.

These predicates are equivalent to math functions found in BASIC, C, Pascal, and so on, but they behave like all predicates in Turbo Prolog. Don't make the mistake of thinking of them procedurally. Remember that values can be instantiated—Prolog can plug in different values attempting to prove the expression true or false—or the value can be bound to the variable, in which case it will succeed or fail under those constraints.

The mathematics predicates fall into five main groups. Logarithmic is one of these, with three member predicates. They are: **log(x)**, which binds **x** to the base-10 logarithm of the original **x**, **ln(x)**, which does the same for the base-*e* logarithm of the beginning value, and **exp(x)**, to bind **x** to the value of *e* raised to the power of the starting value. With these you have all the power of logarithmic manipulation available in a declarative programming environment.

Trigonometric functions are also present. These four predicates are **sin(x)**, to bind the sine of the original value of **x** to **x**, **cos(x)** which does the same for the cosine; **tan(x)**, to handle the tangent; and **arctangent(x)**, which binds **x** to the arctangent of the beginning value of **x**.

There is a miscellaneous group of three predicates: **abs (x)**, to bind the absolute value of **x** to **x**; **sqrt(x)**, which does the same for the square root; and **random(x)**, which binds **x** to a random real number under the constraints of 0 < = **x** < 1 (**x** is less than one but greater than zero). To get a larger random number all you have to do is to multiply the variable by 100 or 1000 or whatever range in which you want the numbers to fall. Multiplying by 100 means they would fall randomly between 1 and 100.

Also in the mathematical predicates are two groups of bit related operations, bit-logic and bit-shift. These are primarily used to program the ports and other hardware of your IBM pc or compatible computer. Except for one, they use a three part argument. The predicates **bitor(x,**

```
      Run       Compile       Edit       Options       Files       Setup       Quit

                              conversion
 Li |enter a binary number 1011101                                      |
/* A|93                                                                 |ello
    |Press the SPACE bar                                                |
pred
    bin_to_dec(string, integer, integer)              |Goal:
    readbin(string)                                   |
                                                      |
goal                                                  |
    readbin(Binary).                                  |
clauses                                               |
                                                      |
    readbin(Binary):-                                 |
        makewindow(1,7,7,"conversion" ,3,5,5,70),     |
        write("enter a binary number "),
                   Message
Load ANS73.PRO
Compiling ANS73.PRO
bin_to_dec
readbin

Use first letter of option  or  select with  ->  or  <-
```

Fig. 10-3. This program reads in a binary number (1011101) and translates it into decimal form (93).

```
   Run      Compile     Edit      Options      Files      Setup      Quit
──────────────────────────────── Editor ────────────────────────────────
  Line 1       Col 1       Indent   Insert   ANS68.PRO
/* Answer to exercise on Page 68 */

predicates
     run
     mysqrt(real,real,real)
     sys_sqrt(real,real)
     equal(real,real)
     get_roots(real,real,real)

goal
     run.

clauses

     run:-
          makewindow(1,7,7,"",15,10,10,60),
          write("Enter a number: "),
          readreal(D),nl,

Use first letter of option  or  select with  ->  or  <-
```

Fig. 10-4. This program (in the ANSWERS subdirectory of the Library and Sample Programs disk) demonstrates how Turbo Prolog can find the square roots of numbers.

y, z), **bitand(x, y, z)** and **bitxor(x, y, z)** take the bound integer values of the first two variables, convert them into 16-bit binary numbers, do the indicated binary operation, and bind the third argument (assuming that it's a free variable not already bound) to that result. The only bit related operation that has only two arguments is **bitnot(x, z)**, which binds **z** to the logical of result of the NOT operation.

The two other bit-field predicates are **bitleft(x, y, z)**, which binds **y** to result of shifting **x** left *n* positions, and **bitright(x, y, z)** doing the same thing to the right. Like the other operations in Prolog, these are not evaluated exactly the same as in a procedural language. You'll need to experiment some to get this down.

Essentially, the bit-field predicates work like this: if the variable is free—not previously bound to some value—the expression being evaluated will instantiate it in an attempt to resolve the subgoal of which it is part. If the variable is bound, Prolog will attempt to balance the arguments and see if they are mathematically correct. If so, the predicate is proved **True**; otherwise it fails.

There is only one way you are going to learn and retain the differences in calculation and other mathematical operations between Prolog and the older procedural languages: Experiment!

RECURSION

Recursion is a very important programming concept in Turbo Prolog. It is used in two situations. The first is when relations are described with the help of the relations themselves. The second is when compound objects are part of other compound objects—they are recursive objects.

The first situation is the one you normally learn in a computer science course, and it is generally introduced as a mathematical technique in evaluating factorials. Recursion, however, has a much wider use, as we shall see shortly. For now, we too will look at factorials.

If you are following along on your computer, load in example program number ten on the Library and Sample Programs disk: EXAMPL10.PRO. This program in simply an implementation of a single user-defined predicate, **factorial(n, f)**, where **n** is a real number used so that answers greater than the integer limit of 32,767 can be returned. Factorials are mathematically a continuing series of products resulting from increasing or decreasing an expression by a constant, generally 1. In this particular predicate, Prolog will find it to be true if:

```
F = N * (N-1) * (N-2) * ... * 3 * 2 * 1
```

Take 4 as an example and plug it into this expression as N. You get 4 * 4 – 1 (or 3) * 2 * 1, which equals 24. Thus, 24 is the factorial of 4. See the recursion? The term N is used to define itself, shifting in value downwards after each evaluation.

Try the sample program. Select Run on the main menu bar. When

```
   Run      Compile      Edit      Options      Files      Setup      Quit

 ----------------------- Editor ---------------------  |TURBO PROLOG version 1.1 |
  Line 1      Col 1      Indent   Insert   WORK.PRO    |--------------------------|
                                                       |Colors                    |
                                                       |Window size               |
                                                       |Directories               |
                                   |PRO     directory  A:ç
                                   |OBJ     directory  A:ç
                                   |EXE     directory  A:ç
                                   |Turbo   directory  A:ç

 ----------------------- Message ---------------------   ---------- Trace ----------

 Compiling WORK.PRO
 Compilation successful

Use first letter of option  or  select with  ->  or  <-
```

Fig. 10-5. When you compile your Turbo Prolog program, be sure things are set up correctly.

asked for a goal, enter **factorial(6, Answer)**. You will get **Answer = 720**, as 720 is the factorial of 6.

Look at the way this factorial rule has been implemented in the clauses section. This rule is:

```
factorial(N, Res) if N > 0 and N1 = N-1 and factorial(N1, FacN1)
  and Res = N*FacN1
```

This rule is broken on several lines in EXAMPL10.PRO to enhance readability, but is still just one rule.

Such mathematical recursive techniques have long been a staple of esoteric computer programming. More practical, however, is the second type of recursion.

RECURSIVE OBJECTS

The second use of recursion is to describe objects where the total number is not known in advance. For example, how can an object be constructed that will describe the names of all members in an organization if we don't know the number of members in advance? Let's build a domains declaration to handle this step by step.

We first devise a domains definition of an empty organization with no members. The entry in the domains section would be **memberlist = empty**. Next we formulate a recursive definition:

```
member(name, memberlist)
```

A typical object (in this case a person who belongs to the group) would be **member(bob, X)**, which symbolizes a membership list with **bob** as the first member, and a smaller list without him. A list with two members would be:

```
member(bob, member(mike, empty))
```

and one with three is:

```
member(bob, member(mike, member(gail, empty)))
```

The predicate **member(name, memberlist)** is a compound object; the functor is an organization, name is one member of that organization; and memberlist has the other members. Finally we have the completed recursive compound object domain declaration, which is really two alternative definitions:

```
memberlist = member(name, memberlist) ; empty
```

Remember that the semicolon is a glue symbol meaning **or**.

You could have the same sort of recursive definition for numbers, as well. An equivalent domain declaration in this case would be:

```
integerlist = list(integer, integerlist) ; empty
```

MAINTAINING CONTROL

One important consideration you will face in using recursive techniques in your programs is maintaining control. In our factorial example, the program stopped when it reached 1. Other recursion operations must have similar limits imposed or they can run away from you, looping until a stack overflow error occurs.

The "stack" is a portion of memory set aside by Turbo Prolog to store the variables and their values that are being used as recursion searches for a solution. While the stack area can be expanded (from 600 to 4000) in the Miscellaneous Settings submenu of the Setup menu, there is still an upper limit that can quickly be reached if your programming is sloppy.

Chapter 11

Lists

LISTS ARE THE BASIC DATA STRUCTURE IN TURBO PROgrams. This is the real foundation of artificial intelligence. In fact, one of Prolog's competitive AI languages, LISP, stands for List Processing.

Because lists are so common in the programs that you will be writing in Turbo Prolog, an easier way to handle them is provided than the compound objects we met first in Chapter 7 and most recently in our discussion of recursion. A list that consists of the series of numbers 1, 2, 3, 4 can be written in Turbo Prolog as [1, 2, 3, 4], separated by commas and enclosed in square brackets. The interior spacing is optional, included here only for enhanced readability.

Symbols may be represented in lists the same way; a list of barnyard animals might be

```
[cow, rooster, pig, sheep, goat]
```

Strings of characters may also be in lists. By enclosing the components of a list in quotes (or the contents of any string variable for that matter) normal use of upper- and lowercase is achieved. Such a list might be of movie stars:

```
["George Burns", "Raquel Welch", "Robert Redford", "Bo Derek"]
```

```
/* Program 12.PRO */

domains
        integerlist = integer*
predicates
        numbers(integerlist)
        write_a_list(integerlist)

clauses
        numbers([1,2,3,4,5,6,7,8,9,10,11,12]).
        write_a_list([]).
        write_a_list([Head|Tail]) if
                write(Head),nl,write_a_list(Tail).
goal
        clearwindow,
        makewindow(1,15,15,"Write A List",0,0,25,80),
        numbers(A),
        write_a_list(A),
        nl,write("(press any key to end)"),
        readchar(Dummy),
        removewindow.
```

Fig. 11-1. Lists are an important part of artificial intelligence.

And, lists can contain lists which contain lists which contain lists, and so on. Some very complex and powerful structures can be erected and manipulated in this manner.

DOMAINS DECLARATION

Setting up a domains declaration for a list is simple. For example, integerlist = integer* will allow you to have a list of integers, or a list of integers which contains other lists of integers. The asterisk indicates that this is a list. While the objects in a list can be anything, including other lists, all the elements of all of these must be the same. You cannot mix strings and symbols, or integers and real numbers, or any other combination.

Also, the declaration must be complete: the element that makes up the list or lists has to be declared. Take the list of movie stars; to set that up, you would need to enter two lines in the domains section of your program. They are: movieStarList = starname* and starName = string. The first sets up a list of string objects, and the second makes those objects strings.

Okay, let's take a quantum leap forward now. The movie star list is a pretty simple example, the earlier one of an integer list even more so. Visualize computer print-outs for a moment—reams of 120-column green-barred paper. How many of them have just one object per line? Very few, that's how many.

In a membership list, for instance, are entries such as Last Name, First Name, Middle Initial, Address, City, State, Zip, Phone Number, Years Member, and probably five or six other things relating to association business, such as dues owed and so forth. Now, how can you cram all this data into one simple object?

The answer: use a compound object!

The general form for declaring domains consisting of compound objects is:

```
myCompDom = f1(d11, ... , d1n) ; f2(d21, ... , d2M); fM(dN1, ... , dNk)
```

The right side of a compound domains declarative can define several alternatives, using a semicolon or the word **or** to separate them. Each of these must have a unique functor and the descriptions for the domains of the actual subcomponents. Expanding our "owners" example, we could have

```
owners = owns(name, book); likes(name, type_of_book);
   listens(name, music_type)
```

and so forth.

To get in all the information we want into each object of the list, we would declare a list consisting of compound objects. The two domains declarations for our membership list would be: **memberlist = member*** (for the list) and

```
memberdata = member(lastName, firstName, MI, address, city,
   state, zip, phone, yearsMember, duesOwed)
```

this being the compound object.

The components of the compound object must also be declared, so we add a third and fourth and fifth domains line:

```
lastName, firstName, MI, address, city, state, zip, phone = string
                     yearsMember = integer
                        duesOwed = real
```

Now we can go on and declare the predicates needed to manipulate the

```
 Run      Compile      Edit      Options      Files      Setup      Quit

------------------------------- Editor -------------------------------
 Line 1      Col 1      Indent  Insert  ANS146.PRO
/* More explanation for example on Page 146 */
/*
  LIST REVERSE
  Enter the goal:
     reverse(•a,b,c,z§,ANS).

*/

domains
     list = symbol*

predicates
     reverse(list,list)
     reverse1(list,list,list)

clauses
     reverse(X,Y):-reverse1(•§,X,Y).
     reverse1(Y,•§,Y).

Use first letter of option  or  select with  ->  or  <-
```

Fig. 11-2. This sample program, which reverses a list, is found on the Library and Sample Programs disk.

list and their related clauses. The list itself must also be entered as a clause.

Remember that just as there can be many levels of lists within a list structure, there may also be many levels of compound objects within a particular compound object. You should have no trouble coming up with a structure to handle even your most complex lists needs.

LIST PROCESSING

Turbo Prolog processes a list by dividing it into a *head* and a *tail*. In the integer list [1, 2, 3, 4], the head is the element 1, and the tail is what is left over, [2, 3, 4]. In predicates that work on lists, a vertical bar | is used to separate the head and tail of a list, in the format head | tail.

The predicate you would define to handle such an integer list as our example would be in the form:

numberLister(head | tail)

Entering the goal numberList(A | B) causes the variable A to be bound to the head of the list and B is bound to the rest.

Logic operations apply here as elsewhere in Turbo Prolog. The goal numberLister([1 | B]) returns a True because 1 is the head of that particular list. Now, let's move on to a list containing names.

Sample program number 11 (EXAMPL11.PRO) on the "Library and Sample Programs" disk is a good introduction to the techniques used in manipulating a membership list. It is based on the predicate **member(name, namelist)**, where "name" is a symbol and **namelist** is a simple list made up of the object **name**.

In this program, as in almost all Turbo Prolog programs, we have the domains, predicates, and clauses sections. The domain declarations are easy, **namelist = name*** and **name = symbol**. The predicate **member(name,namelist) is the only entry in the predicates section. It expresses the relationship, member**, between a particular name and the rest of the list.

Next, under clauses, come the two rules that will determine how the list is handled. The first is:

```
member(Name, [Name | _]).
```

Remember that a clause must be terminated with a period and variables started with an uppercase letter. The underline character refers to a blank variable, one that could be any value. It's used more or less as a place marker.

In this particular clause, the head of the list is examined to see if the name is there; the tail is ignored. The goal

```
member(john, [john, charlie, joe_bob, marvin])
```

comes back **True** because John is the head of the list. The goal

```
member(john,[herman, mary, susie, john, pignose])
```

is false because John is not the head of the list.

In this case we need a second clause to examine the rest of the list to see if John is there. This is done with the second clause in EXAMPL11.PRO:

```
member(Name, [_ |Tail]) if member(Name,Tail).
```

Translating this to English, the logic is, "**Name** is a member of the list if **Name** is a member of the tail." The program examines the individual objects in the tail part of the list for a match; if **John** is found, a **True** is returned.

WRITING PARTS OF A LIST

True and false returns are nice in logic programming, but more

```
    Run      Compile     Edit     Options     Files     Setup     Quit

                              Editor
  Line 1      Col 1      Indent  Insert  ANS135.PRO
/* Answer to exercise on Page 135 */
/*
  The append program for complex lists. This is an
  advanced technique. Please read the "Fascinating
  Worlds of Lists and Recursion " and "Basic Language
  Elements" in your manual.

  Complex lists are handled by the following domain
  declarations. A list must have a functor as shown
  and then must be declared recursively.
*/

domains
  llist = l(list) ; s(symbol) ; i(integer) ; c(char) ; t(string)
  list = llist*

predicates
   append(list,list,list)

Use first letter of option  or  select with -> or <-
```

Fig. 11-3. Turbo Prolog techniques for appending lists are very powerful.

realistically you want solid data in reply to your requests. If you ask, "Is Bob Q. Jones a member?" you would like the program to return something like "Jones, Bob Q., 1804 Dogbite Lane, Poodlepuke, NY 01234, (212) 555-1212, member 8 years, dues owed = $15." Using recursive techniques you can define a predicate to write out the elements of a list on separate lines or in whatever format you may need.

The Turbo Prolog *Owner's Handbook* gives an example that works well and is a good starting point for elaboration into one fitting your particular applications. It consists of two clauses. The first is **write_a_list([ ])**. Essentially, this clause tells the program to "stop when there are no more elements to write." The second:

```
write(Head), nl, write_a_list(Tail).
```

means: "Write the head of the list, write a new line, and then deal with the tail." If the object is compound, it can do all the components of the object, or just those you have specified.

Let's do a sample program of our own to demonstrate the practical implementation of writing a list. The domains declaration is for a list of integers and is: **integerlist = integer***. Since it's standard type and we're not calling the elements of the list anything else, this is all we have to do for domains. In the predicates section we have two predicates—**numbers(integerlist)**, which defines the clause that will contain the list of numbers, and write_a_list(interlist), that will actually cause the list of numbers to be displayed on the screen, one per line.

In the clauses section are three:

```
numbers([1, 2, 3, 4, 5, 6, 7, 8, 9, 10, 11, 12]).
```

which contains our number list. The second,

```
write_a_list([ ]).
```

is used to stop operation when all the elements of the list have been written out. The third and last clause:

```
write_a_list([Head | Tail]) if write(Head), nl, write_a_list(Tail).
```

is the recursive rule that writes out the list one member per line.

First in the goal section is a clearwindow predicate. This is one of Turbo Prolog's built-in predicates (hence requiring no predicates declaration) and does nothing more than clear your computer's screen. The second subgoal is:

```
makewindow (1, 15, 15, "Write A List", 0, 0, 25, 80).
```

Another of the built-in predicates, it causes a window to be created on the screen, into which we will write the elements of the list.

The window predicate consists of three numbers, a string, and then four more numbers. These are what determine the size and color of the window. The first number inside the parentheses, a 1 in this case, is the number of the window, giving you a way to jump from window to window if you have more than one on the screen. The second number is the color attribute of the window itself. We have 15 here, which is bright white on black. If it were 78, it would be bright yellow on red; 23 is white on blue. These color attributes are exactly the same as you find anywhere in MS-DOS CGA (color graphics adapter) programming. The next number determines the color of the window's frame. We also have it bright white on black.

The string in quotes is the title of the window. Entering a null string (" ") here will cause no title to appear. The next two numbers specify the starting point of the window, point 0,0, in this case, which is the very first top left-most point on your screen. The last two designate the size of the window, with 25 lines 80 columns wide being the maximum. The windowing system in Turbo Prolog lets you write some very slick-appearing programs.

The next to last subgoal is number(A). All this does is bind the in-

```
|     Run     Compile     Edit     Options     Files     Setup     Quit     |

------------------------------ Editor ------------------------------
|  Line 1     Col 1     Indent  Insert  EXAMPL29.PRO                     |
|/* Program 29 */                                                        |
|                                                                        |
|domains                                                                 |
|     list=symbol*                                                       |
|     scores=integer                                                     |
|                                                                        |
|predicates                                                              |
|     member(symbol,list)                                                |
|     run                                                                |
|     continue(list,scores)                                              |
|     yes_no_count(symbol,list)                                          |
|     guessword(scores,list)                                             |
|     word(list,integer)                                                 |
|     read_as_list(list,integer)                                         |
|                                                                        |
|goal                                                                    |
|     makewindow(1,7,0,"",0,0,25,80),                                    |
|     makewindow(2,7,135,"Counting",1,20,4,34),                          |
Use first letter of option  or  select with  ->  or  <-
```

Fig. 11-4. Example program 29 is a good introduction to list manipulation.

teger list to the variable A, making use of our first predicate declaration. And the last subgoal, **write_a_list(A)**, is the one that does the real work. It causes the list to be written out, one number per line.

Running this program causes a window to appear which covers the whole screen, and the list is printed to the screen within it. Since the goals are now internal and none of them ask for input, you do not have to enter anything.

You can now compile this into a stand-alone, executable program. To do this, return to the main menu bar and invoke the Options submenu. Choose the "EXE file (auto link)" option.You will be returned automatically to the main menu bar. Now simply choose compile and the program will be quickly compiled and a stand-alone version created. If you named this particular program "12.PRO," as I did, the stand-alone program will be 12.EXE, and to run it from DOS all you have to do is to type **12**. Works great!

APPENDING LISTS

Back to sample program number 11; the "member" predicate works in two ways. Let's look at the pair of clauses it defines again:

member(Name | _]).

and

```
member(Name, [_ | Tail]) if member(Name, Tail).
```

From a declarative point of view, these two clauses say that, given a list, **Name** is a member of that list if its head is **Name**; if not, then **Name** is found to be a member of the list if it belongs to the tail of the list. **True** or **False** is returned.

From a practical standpoint, we are most often looking for actual data rather than a logical yes or no. So a more procedurally oriented result is usually wanted. We will get a procedural result declaratively; which brings us to the second way of using these two clauses. From a procedural viewpoint the two clauses can be interpreted as, "To find a member of a list, find its head; otherwise find a member of its tail." This returns a result in the form of actual data.

In the two clauses above, it depends on how we state the goal that determines how they are used. The goal

```
member(2, [1, 2, 3, 4]
```

is declarative, and asks if "2" is a member of the list. It is found to be so and **True** is returned. The goal

```
member(X, [1, 2, 3, 4]
```

however, fits the second case. Here we get actual data back in the form of the list itself, in the variable "X."

Often if we construct clauses from the declarative point of view, they will also work procedurally in Turbo Prolog. Let's look at an example of this by constructing a predicate that will append one list to another. Since we are hot on the integer list right now, we'll append one of those to another.

Logically, three lists are involved: the original list, the one to be appended, and the new list, that is a combination of the first two. The predicate we define to do this job will be in the general form:

```
append (List1, List2, List3)
```

This will combine **List1** and **List2** to give us **List3**. Again, we are using recursion, from a procedural point of view.

In actual operation, if **List1** is empty, this is the same as making **List3** equal to **List2**. Sample program number 12 (EXAMPL12.PRO) contains an example of this. The predicate that performs the action if **List1** is empty is

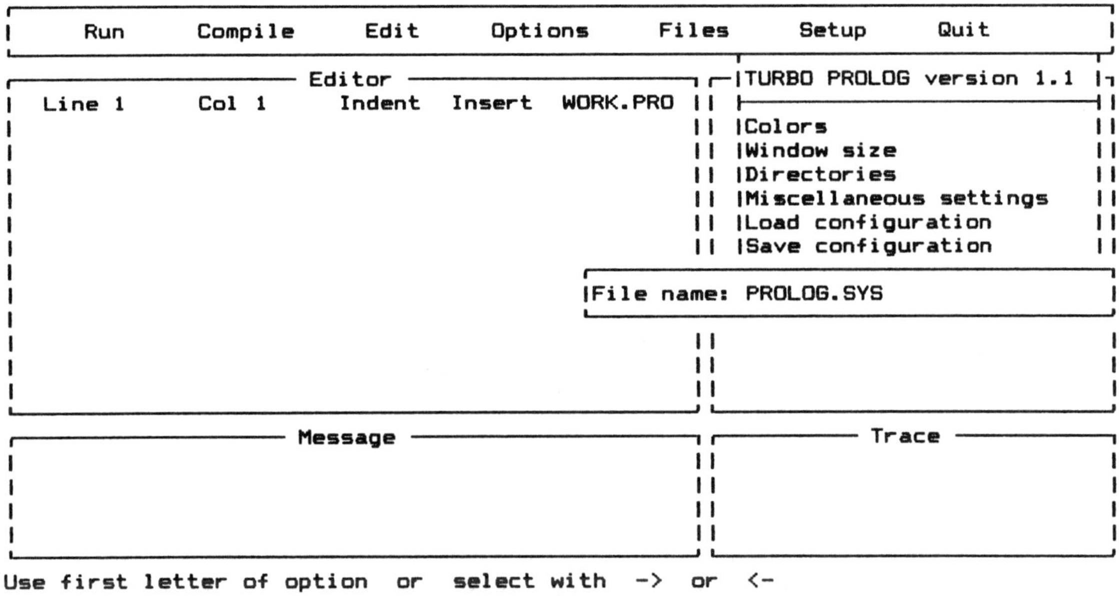

Fig. 11-5. You can have as many configuration files for the programming environment as you wish.

append([ ]), List, List).

On the other hand, assuming **List1** has something in it, the combination takes place by making the head of **List1** the head of **List3**. The rest of **List3** (its tail) is obtained by combining the rest of **List1** and all of **List2**. The predicate that handles this is written:

append([X | L1], List2, [X | L3]) if append(L1, List2, L3).

If you are following along on your computer, load EXAMPLE12.PRO, take a look at it, then run it and enter the goal

append ([1, 2, 3], [4, 5, 6], L) and writelist (L).

The **writelist** predicate is the same as the **write_a_list** one we looked at above. The goal just given will not only combine those two lists, it will write them out to the screen as well. Try it out, and experiment with modification. Just be sure, if you get something neat and want to save it, to do it under a different name so you won't wipe out EXAMPLE12.PRO.

Chapter 12

Files and Strings

FILES AND STRINGS ARE THE MAIN WAY TURBO PROLOG OBTAINS and stores data—either from or to permanent storage, using the MS-DOS filing structure or for internal data manipulation by the use of strings. A *string* is nothing more than a series of mixed letters, numbers and spaces enclosed with quotes.

A *file* is a collection of program steps or other data, recorded on a floppy disk or hard disk. These files are separately named entities, the name being a unique series of letters and/or numbers. Under MS-DOS you may have file names up to eight characters long with a period and an extension of three more characters. File names in Turbo Prolog are different, even when referring to an MS-DOS file name. We'll discuss these *symbolic* names in detail shortly.

PROLOG.EXE, the program that creates the Turbo Prolog programming environment in your computer, is a file of machine-readable program steps that instructs your computer how to set up the environment for you and compile your text into programs. It's called a *binary* file. README, on the other hand, is a *text* file, describing the latest changes implemented in your particular version of Prolog.

At first, the data files you create and use with Turbo Prolog will all be text files. All the example program files and those you write and save will be text files, as well. Turbo Prolog is chock full of file and string-handling predicates. We'll divide these up and look at them in logical families.

FILE SYSTEM

The standard built-in predicates for the reading and writing of files are very elegant and efficient, especially when compared to equivalent procedural methods in BASIC. A single one of these file-related predicates can cause output to be routed to a file instead of being displayed on the screen.

Turbo Prolog programs make use of a **current_read_device**, from which input is accepted, and a **current_write_device**, to which output is sent. Usually your computer's keyboard is the input device, and the screen is the write device to which output is "written."

To type in each data entry and write down the answers that scroll up on the screen is not the time saving, automatic work concept of computing, so Turbo Prolog gives you a host of other options. For instance, you could instruct the program to obtain its data from a file stored externally on floppy or hard disk, and to write the answers to a printer.

The program can shift around the combination of input and output devices as needed, whether in a preset pattern that you've determined the logic far ahead of time, or in response to various data "stimuli." Whatever you choose, reading and writing is handled identically within a Turbo Prolog program.

The underlying principle of using a data file is the same in Turbo Prolog as it is in BASIC or Pascal. The file must first be opened. A number of files may be open at any one time. The number of these depends mainly on the contents of your CONFIG.SYS file, on the disk you use to initialize your computer from power-off.

A file may be opened in one of four ways: for reading from, for writing to, for appending to, or for modification (i.e., editing). A file that is

```
Help

        STANDARD PREDICATES

INPUT
=====
file_str(DosFileName,StringVariable)    File <---> String
        (string,string) -- (inp,outp)  (inp,inp)

inkey(CharVariable)
        (Char) -- (outp)

keypressed

readchar(CharVariable)
        (char) -- (outp)

readint(IntgVariable)
        (integer) -- (outp)
```

Fig. 12-1. File_str, a very powerful predicate, is shown here in the help window.

opened for any other reason than reading from *must* be closed when that activity is finished or the changes will be lost.

The best technique is to open several files at once so data input and output can be quickly redirected to them; opening and closing files takes awhile. *But* if a file receives important data and won't be used while other functions are being done, you should close it immediately. Anything amiss, such as the power blipping out, the user aborting the program, or a "bug" doing so during a later operation, will cause the changes to all opened files to be lost.

When you open a file, Turbo Prolog connects a *symbolic* file name to the actual file name used by MS-DOS. Symbolic files names are the ones you will use to redirect input and output. They have to start with a lowercase letter. Also, these names must be declared in the domains section of your program, with the further restriction that only one line of file declarations is allowed—although a number of symbolic names may be declared here using the semicolon to glue them together, as in:

```
files = file1; source; auxiliary
```

However, there are also four built-in "files" which do not have to be declared and which are used for routing to devices other than on a floppy or hard disk. These are printer, screen, keyboard, and com1.

Printer is pretty obvious: it routes output to the printer or to what-

```
                                  Help
STRING HANDLING
===============
concat(String1,String2,String3)   String3 = String1 + String2
         (string,string,string) -- (inp,inp,outp) (inp,outp,inp)
         (outp,inp,inp) (inp,inp,inp)

frontchar(String,FrontChar,RestString)
         (string,char,string) -- (inp,outp,outp) (inp,inp,outp)
         (inp,outp,inp) (inp,inp,inp) (outp,inp,inp)

frontstr(Lenght,Inpstring,StartString,RestString)
         (integer,string,string,string) -- (inp,inp,outp,outp)

fronttoken(String,Token,RestString)
         (string,string,string) -- (inp,outp,outp) (inp,inp,outp)
         (inp,outp,inp) (inp,inp,inp) (outp,inp,inp)

isname(StringParam)
         (string) -- (inp)

str_len(String,Length)
         (string,integer) -- (inp,inp) (inp,outp)
```

Fig. 12-2. Basic formats for string handling predicates.

```
     Run      Compile      Edit      Options      Files      Setup      Quit

                                  Editor              Dialog
 Line 1      Col 1      Indent  Insert  EXAMPL56.P  |pword
/* Program 56 */                                     |Division: a-verylongmadeupwo
/*                                                   |rd
 This program attempts to divide words into          |Division: ave-rylongmadeupwo
 syllables.                                          |rd
*/                                                   |Division: avery-longmadeupwo
                                                     |rd
domains                                              |Division: averylongma-deupwo
    letter = char                                    |rd
    word = letter*                                   |Division: averylongmadeup-wo
                                                     |rd
predicates                                           |
    divide(word,word,word,word)                      |Press the SPACE bar
    vocal(letter)
    consonant(letter)
    string_word(string,word)
    append(word,word,word)

goal
Use first letter of option  or  select with  ->  or  <-
```

Fig. 12-3. This program to divide words into syllables is a basic example of string manipulation.

ever device might be hooked to the parallel LPT1: port. Since output can be further redirected in the initial MS-DOS set-up, this can add considerable flexibility.

The second predefined file, **screen**, routes data to the computer screen. It is also possible to get input this way. The **keyboard** file is also readily apparent, and is an input device.

The last predefined symbolic file, **com1**, is the first serial port on an IBM PC or compatible computer. A wide variety of devices may be interfaced here: modems to attach the computer to the phone lines, plotters to draw diagrams, digital-to-analog converters which convert computer data to real-world devices like numerical control machine tools or switches that control heating and lighting in your home and accept their input back, and much more. Being able to send output and accept input to **com1** opens up possibilities for artificial intelligence programs, including controlling robotic devices.

The predicates used for routing are:

```
readdevice (SymbolicFileName)
```

for input, and

```
writedevice (SymbolicFileName)
```

for output. The symbolic file name can be any of the four predefined ones, or any name you declare on the **files** = . . . line of your domains declarations. Remember, too, that such indications as **SymbolicFileName** refers to a variable (starting with uppercase) which is bound to the value you want to be the argument of the predicate.

There are four ways to open files on floppy or hard disk, so there are four corresponding simple predicates to handle opening and one to close already opened files. You will be using these a lot.

The first is opening files for reading. The general format of this predefined predicate is:

```
openread (SymbolicFileName, DosFileName)
```

Say, for example, you are maintaining the membership list for your local Loyal Order of Moose. The names and addresses are all recorded in a physical file on disk named **moosemem.dta**. You want to open this file and print out a membership list for the secretary to use in sending out the newsletter. The first step is to open the file to read and assign a symbolic file name which can be routed to the printer in a later step.

The symbolic file name can be anything you choose though a descriptive term can be less confusing should you or someone else later want to modify the program. You might decide to use **namesAndAddress** for the symbolic name. Remember, as long as Turbo Prolog names start with lowercase, you are free to mix in uppercase to enhance readability. You are not limited to the eight-character plus three-character extension of MS-DOS file names.

Putting it all together in the predicate to open this file for reading, we get:

```
openread (namesAndAddresses, "moosemem.dta")
```

Please note that the MS-DOS file name is enclosed in quotation marks because it is a *string*, not a Prolog "names." The predicate can be placed either in a clause or as a subgoal in your goal, internal or external.

In an actual program, one that maintains the Moose club list, you would probably want to open this file early to read and leave it open. You would want to do a lot more with it than just print the contents. There would be predicates that told which members owed dues and others to perform various statistical operations on the membership rolls.

The next predicate opens a file to both reading and writing. Since doing so deletes any existing file of that name, you would not want to use this predicate on the Moose membership! But you could *read* from the membership file and *write* to another file all past due members. In this case, you would use the predicate

```
openwrite(SymbolicFileName, DosFileName)
```

```
      Run        Compile       Edit       Options       Files       Setup       Quit
------------------------------ Editor ------------------------------
  Line 1      Col 1      Indent   Insert   EXAMPL59.PRO
/* Program 59 */

include "exampl58.pro"   /*excluding the goal*/

domains
     row,col,length=integer
     field=f(row,col,length)
     position=pos(row,col)

predicates
     scr(field,position,key)

goal
     Row=10,Col=10,Length=30,
     makewindow(1,23,1,"Simple Editor",0,0,25,80),
     write("Edit the text.çnUse the arrow keys to move"),nl,
     write("Hit the F10 key when done"),
     cursor(Row,Col),

Use first letter of option  or  select with  ->  or  <-
```

Fig. 12-4. Word processing is an important use for string manipulation, as shown in this rudimentary editor included with your Turbo Prolog package.

in this manner:

openwrite(pastDueMembers, "pastdue.mem")

Note that a different MS-DOS file name is specified because it is a new file. Also, you must close this file after it is written to actually complete the saving of the data to floppy or hard disk. This is accomplished with the closefile(SymbolicFileName) predefined predicate.

Third, we have the predicate

openappend(SymbolicFileName, DosFileName)

which opens a file for appending or adding to a physical file. We might use this to add new members to the Moose membership list. They would not be in alphabetical order, but a separate sorting operation would take care of that. Again, the file must be closed after the appending operations to permanently record the additions.

And last, we have the predicate

openmodify(SymbolicFileName, DosFileName)

This means that the MS-DOS file is opened for modification. Relating to BASIC, this means that a random access file can be manipulated using the **filepos** predicate to call and update single records, rather than having to read and write an entire sequential file. This is the technique you would really use to maintain the Moose membership list, or any similar application.

The format of the predicate for file position is

```
filepos(SymbolicFileName, FilePosition, Mode)
```

The latter variable, **Mode**, contains the numbers zero, one, or two. The significance of these are: 0 = relative to the start of the file, 1 = relative to the current position, and 2 = relative to the end of the file. Like most Turbo Prolog predicates, they can be used either bound or instantiated. Thus, if **FilePosition** is bound to 24 and **Mode** is bound to zero, the next position written or read will be at position 24 from the start of the file. If **FilePosition** is free, however, it will be instantiated to the particular position at which the file pointer now is.

Be aware, in designing your programs, that whenever a file is assigned as a write device, that all operations will be written to that file until the program encounters a **writedevice** predicate reassigning the output route. So, again, plan the logic of your programs carefully. In this respect, declarative programming can approach procedural programming in flow control, if not in the actual specification of steps needed to implement it as you do in BASIC, C, Pascal, and the others.

One other caution; if the program is running on a computer that doesn't have, for example, a serial port card, or has a printer which is not turned on, errors can result. As in any type of programming, error-trapping must be instituted. It is not professional to have a program bomb because the user forgot to turn on the printer.

Since you certainly don't want your programs to inadvertently open an already existing data file for writing, thus losing its contents, a built-in predicate is supplied to check for these. It's **existfile(DosFileName)**, and it succeeds if the named file is in the currently chosen MS-DOS directory. It fails if the name does not appear in the directory, or if the name is invalid, or if it contains a wild card designator.

You will want to use this predicate to provide another level of protection in your programs: to check a file's existence before trying to open it. A sequence of two clauses will do this, and you can elaborate from there. Remember, these clause rules are constructed, not predefined, so you will have to declare them in the predicates section of you program. The first,

```
open(File, Name):- existfile(Name), !, openread(File, Name).
```

```
     Run      Compile      Edit      Options      Files      Setup      Quit

─────────────────────── Editor ──────┬─────────── Dialog ───────────
  Line 1     Col 1     Indent  Insert  EXAMPL49.P|
/* program 49 */                                 |
/*                                               |
  This program demonstrates findall              |
*/                                               |This program finds the
                                                 |average age from three
domains                                          |lists  with findall.
     name,address = string                       |
     age =integer                                |Average = 43
     list =age*                                  |
                                                 |
predicates                                       |
     person(name,address,age)                    |Press the SPACE bar
     sumlist(list,age,integer)                   |
                                                  
goal
     findall(Age,Person(_,_,Age),L),sumlist(L,Sum,N),
     Ave=Sum/N,
     write("çnçnThis program finds the çnaverage age from three çnlists  with f
Use first letter of option  or  select with  ->  or  <-
```

Fig. 12-5. Example program 49 demonstrates the find all standard predicate.

uses the *cut* to force success if the MS-DOS file is present, by not allowing Turbo Prolog to access the **openread** predicate. If the file does not exist (the condition we actually want), the program moves on to the **openread** predicate and succeeds by opening the file.

The second clause rule is simply to document the fact if the file wasn't found and makes use of a blank variable in doing so. It is:

open(__,File):- write("Error: the file ",Name," is not found.").

If you were checking to see if the file **moosemem.dta** was there, and it is not the clause will write out, **Error, the file moosemem.dta is not found.**

You probably would not want to burden the user with this, and just use the first clause rule to make sure he or she doesn't wipe out their data.

A new file handling-predicate for accessing binary files was added to Turbo Prolog Version 1.1; its format is:

filemode(SymbolicFileName, FileMode)

where **FileMode** is an integer of zero (text mode) or one (binary mode). *Text mode* means that the return character (ASCII 13, causes a carriage return) is suppressed using standard input routines like **readln** and **readchar**. A Return will be inserted before each line feed character during output. *Binary mode* means that no transformations will be done at all. The standard predicates will work normally in this mode.

Two more useful file-handling predicates:

```
deletefile(DosFileName)
```

and

```
renamefile(OldDosFileName, NewDosFileName)
```

The first deletes a physical MS-DOS file, if it's in the current directory, and the second allows you to rename MS-DOS files.

Here's another very useful predefined predicate, especially for those of us lucky enough to have a hard disk. It's **disk(DosPath)**. If bound to a value, such as **C:\prolog**, this predicate will set the directory path to that value. If it's unbound, the current DOS path will be bound to the variable.

STRING PROCESSING

Like files, Turbo Prolog has several built-in predicates which allow you and your programs to manipulate strings. A *string* is simply any collection of characters and numbers bounded by quotes. A string variable in Turbo Prolog may be up to 64K long. That's somewhere over 12,000 words!

The string variable domain type is one that you will find yourself using a lot in storing and working with words and sentences.

There are four uses of special characters in strings that you should know. These involve the backslash followed by one of three letters or another backslash. The first use, (**\n**), a backslash followed immediately with a lowercase n, will cause a new line to be printed when the string is displayed or routed to a printer.

The combination of an embedded **\t** will cause the output to tab and **\b** is a backspace. Which brings us to the fourth. Since MS-DOS makes use of the backslash, especially in directory paths, there has to be some way of causing it to print without trying to force some other action. This is done by simply putting another backslash in front, as in \\.

Example program numbers 46 (EXAMPL46.PRO), 47 (EXAMPL47), and 48 (EXAMPL48.PRO) on the "Library and Sample Programs" disk are demonstrations of how string manipulation is accomplished. Let's look at some of the predicates used to accomplish these tasks—which include dividing a string either into a list of individual characters or into a list of corresponding symbols.

The first predicate, one for string handling built into Turbo Prolog, is:

frontchar(String1, CharParam, String2).

This predicate acts as if it were defined by the equation:

String1 = (the concatenation of CharParam and String2).

The two string variables are just that, while **CharParam** is a **char** domain type variable—it can just hold one letter at a time.

Call up Turbo Prolog, or if you already have it running, Zap the file out of the editor window. Select Run on the main menu bar.

The dialog window will become active and the word **Goal**: appears. Type in the predicate this way: **frontchar("test",A,B).**, and hit Return. What you will get is **A=t, B=est** and below that, **1 Solution**. We have invoked the **frontchar** predicate in the instantiated open, open (i,o,o) flow, pattern. Turbo Prolog put the first character of the string "test" in A and the remainder of the string in B. This should start giving you some ideas on how to use it in programs.

In EXAMPLE46.PRO on the "Library and Sample Programs" disk, **frontchar** is used to define a predicate that changes a string to a list or characters or (depending on the goal you give it) the other way around—taking a list of characters and making a string out of them. The ability to disassemble and reassemble a string piecemeal is a useful technique to have.

The *Owner's Handbook* suggests you start with **string__chlist("ABC",Z)** where ABC is a string and Z is the variable that receives the character list.

Here are some tips: after the **frontchar** predicate, put in the predicate **write(H)** on the same line or the next. This will show you the contents of **CharParam** as Turbo Prolog steps through **String1** in search of a solution to the goal. Try changing the write predicate to S, H, and T, and see what you get. Note also the use of the vertical bar in the **string__chlist** clause rule. What are we doing here? Looking at the head and tail of a list.

The next string-handling predicate is **fronttoken**, and it's used to split a string into a list of tokens. A *token* is nothing more than a Turbo Prolog name, an unsigned number (real or integer), or any non-space character. The general format for this predicate is:

fronttoken(String1, SymbolParam, Rest)

If **fronttoken** is called with **String1** bound, containing a value, it finds the first token of **String1**, which is then returned in the variable **SymbolParam**. The rest of the string is returned in the third variable, **Rest**. Blank spaces are ignored.

A sequence of characters are grouped as one token when it is one of the following: a name according to normal Turbo Prolog syntax (any continous group of lowercase and uppercase letters, numbers, and underline characters that start with a lowercase letter), a number (any preceding sign is returned as a separate token), or a non-space character. Such predicates as **is_name(StringParam)**, can be used to test to see if the token is a name (if not, a number or non-space character), **str_int(StringParam, IntParam)**, binds **StringParam** to a string of digits representing the value of **IntParam**, and **str_len(String, Length)**, binds **Length** to the number of characters in the string.

EXAMPL7.PRO and EXAMPL48.PRO on the "Library and Sample Programs" disk demonstrate the use of the **fronttoken** built-in predicate, and how you can use it to construct specialized, powerful predicates of your own.

Among the other string manipulating predicates is:

```
frontstr(NumberOfChars, String1, StartStr, String2)
```

The four arguments of this predicate are domain types integer, string, string, and string. It works like this: if you bind **NumberOfChars** to an integer and **StarStr** to a string, this will cause Turbo Prolog to return a string of that many characters from the beginning of the starting string and the rest of the original string will be in **String2**.

Also very useful is

```
concat(String1, String2, Longstring)
```

The name *concat* is short for concatenation. In operation, it means that **String3** is obtained by concatenation (joining together) of **String1** and **String2**. At least two of these parameters must be bound before the predicate is invoked, which means it only gives one solution. As an example:

```
concat("the last train to ", "Clarkesville", TrainSchedule)
```

will combine the first two strings, concatenate them, and bind the value to the variable **TrainSchedule**. So **TrainSchedule** now has a value of "the last train to Clarkesville."

Once you have the data, often some sort of conversion is necessary. If you take a string completely apart, all you have left are characters. The string and char domains are not compatible. Or, there may be numbers in the string that you want to convert to integers or real numbers and act on arithmetically.

TYPE CONVERSIONS

Like Pascal, Turbo Prolog is strongly "typed" language. These types are called domains. Domains specify the types of values that objects may take in relation to one another.

Typing solves problems but it can also cause them. Often it becomes necessary to transfer data from one variable domain to another. Turbo Prolog handles this by providing standard built-in predicates to convert between a character and its ASCII value, a string and a character, a string and an integer, a string and a real number, and uppercase and lowercase characters. These predicates, respectively, are:

```
char_ascii(ACharacter, AnInteger)

str_char(OneCharInAString, One Character)

str_int(AString, AnInteger)

str_real(AString, AReal)

upper_lower(UppercaseStr, LowerCaseStr)
```

Conversions between the symbol and string domain types and between integer and real numbers are handled automatically when using predefined predicates.

You do not have to use the same variable names given here and in the *Owner's Handbook*. You can use A and B or X and Y or Fred and Fatima. For you own convenience and understanding, however, it is better to use descriptive names.

THE FINDALL PREDICATE

The built-in predicate "**findall**" may not seem at first blush to belong in a chapter about files and string manipulations, but this feature sees heavy use in the processing of strings and lists.

Findall is used to collect specified values by backtracking through a list or a string converted to a list, either through tokens, or by stripping the characters and making them into a list. The general form for this predicate is:

```
findall(VarName, yourpredicate(. . .),ListParam)
```

The first parameter tells Turbo Prolog which variable designates the values to be collected in a list, the second is a predicate of your own construction that provides multiple values in the backtracking process, and the last is a variable that holds the list of values from backtracking. There must be a domain defined by you to which all the values of **ListParam** belong. EXAMPL49.PRO on the "Library and Sample Programs" disk demonstrates the use of **findall**, and how you can use it to construct specialized, powerful predicates of your own.

Chapter 13

Reading and Writing, Windows and Graphics

THIS CHAPTER COULD JUST AS WELL BE ENTITLED "INPUT AND Output." It's about the various ways in which Turbo Prolog obtains and prints out information to screen and printer. We will look at regular text and graphics modes.

Let's think about software from the viewpoint of the end user for a moment. Programmers become bemused with the elegant logic of our programs, the little nuances in coding that makes this or that run ever so smoother. The general computer user is not impressed by that. They notice the amateurish grammar and the misspellings. They groan in frustration at trying to make sense of the jumbled, hard-to-read screens. To succeed as any kind of programmer, your programs must be cosmetically attractive. Turbo Prolog's various reading, writing, windowing, screen-handling, and graphics predicates make this easy for you.

The foundation for developing and building your software written with Turbo Prolog is the *windows* system. I am not talking about the programming environment windows such as edit, dialog, trace, and message, but the windows created at run-time. These are ones that you can specify, manipulate, and cause to have moved about blazingly fast and rainbow-colored. This is how you can really dazzle the end user and have him or her convinced of your programming wizardry.

WRITING

We have already met the basic output predicate, **write**. The **write** predicate, like most of those in Turbo Prolog, has an inherent flow pattern. Flow patterns are described in the "Alphabetical Index of Standard Predicates," which starts on page 181 of the Turbo Prolog *Owner's Handbook*. The "i" means "instantiated" or bound to a value, and "o" stands for "open," not bound to a specific value.

In the case of **write**, you have the option of only one flow pattern, **(i*)**. The asterisk indicates an optional number of arguments. This means that before you write out a variable, to the screen, printer, a file, or wherever, you must first cause it to be bound to a value. As an example, the two steps **A = 3** and **write(A)** would cause **3** to appear on the computer screen, that being the default write device. If you entered **write(A)** without first instantiating it to a value, an error message results.

The format for this predicate is:

```
write(e, e2, e3, ... , eN)
```

where the given constants or values are written in the active window on the current write device. It can be called with an optional number of arguments (**ei**), which are either constants or variables bound to the standard domain types of real, integer, char, string, or symbol. Just remember that the value of the variable must be bound before the **write** predicate is invoked.

Used with **write** is the *newline*, **nl**, predicate. This is one of the few predicates in all of Turbo Prolog that does not have any arguments, and is thus neither instantiated nor open. It is exactly the same as hitting the carriage return on that old electric typewriter you junked in favor of electronic word processing. The output of your programs must have **nl** embedded at appropriate places or the text on the screen will be jum-

```
---------------------------------- Help ----------------------------------
WINDOW SYSTEM
=============
clearwindow()

gotowindow(WindowNo)
        (integer) -- (inp)

makewindow(WindowNo,ScrAtt,FrameAtt,Framestr,Row,Column,Height,Width)
        (integer,integer,integer,string,integer,integer,integer,integer)
        -- (inp,inp,inp,inp,inp,inp,inp,inp)
           (outp,outp,outp,outp,outp,outp,outp,outp)

removewindow()

scroll(RowsToScroll,ColsToScroll)
        (integer,integer) -- (inp,inp)

shiftwindow(WindowNo)
        (integer) -- (inp) (outp)

window_str(ScreenString)
        (string) -- (inp) (outp)
```

Fig. 13-1. Here are some of the window predicates in the help window.

bled and break at odd places.

In a program, **write(ThisVariable, ThatVariable), nl** will write the previously bound **ThisVariable** and **ThatVariable** joined together on a single line and cause a carriage return. Now let's add a modicum of sophistication. What if we wanted a space between the two variables, or a comma, or a dash or an embedded comment? Use the variables in a sentence with the constants like this:

```
write("In making an omelet, you will need ", ThisVariable, "and",
   ThatVariable, ".")
```

The variables, of course, would be bound to string or symbol values such as **eggs** and **milk**.

The predicates **write** and **nl** will become old and familiar friends. They are used more than any other predicate in Turbo Prolog.

CONTROLLING WRITE OUTPUT

We met the **writedevice** predicate in the last chapter. It specifies where the **write** predicate sends its output. Like most Turbo Prolog variables, this one has a flow pattern attached; in this case it is either instantiated or open. Thus, the predicate works in one of two ways.

Instantiated, as in **writedevice(Variable)**, the current write device will be reassigned to the symbolic file name in **Variable**. This name may represent an actual MS-DOS file already opened for writing or modifying, or it may be one of the predefined "files" such as **screen, printer**, and **com1**.

If **Variable** is open, however, when the **writedevice** predicate is invoked, **Variable** will be bound to the value of whatever the current write device is. The difference between these two uses of this predicate is important to understand. In the first, the program changes the output device—perhaps from the screen to the printer. In the second, we are asking "what is the current output device?" From the value returned to the variable we can cause decisions to be made.

If output were to the printer instead of the screen, you would want to include paging parameters and the like. You can not know in every instance what output device the end user will be employing. **Writedevice** is simply one of the many predicates that allow the program to know what's going on and make the appropriate decisions.

The **writef** predicate is available to "pretty print" groups of variables. The general format for the predicate is:

```
writef(FormatString, Arg1, Arg2, Arg3, ...)
```

Like the **write** predicate itself, the number of arguments are options. And the only flow pattern allowed is instantiated values.

This predicate will produce a formatted output if **Arg1** to **ArgN** are constants or variables belonging to the standard domains. The procedures here is somewhat analogous to the PRINT USING function in BASIC, but more flexible and powerful. Like PRINT USING, it provides a "mask" to control the number of decimal places in printing variables. But—heh, heh—let's see you embed carriage returns in a PRINT USING command in BASIC! Using **writef** in Turbo Prolog you can do this, and more.

The first argument of the predicate, **FormatString**, is where your control specifiers for the rest of the arguments to. The other arguments are variables of the standard domains. The form for the specifier string is %– **m.p**. The values in this form may have been previously bound to **FormatString** or you may simply include it inside quotes in the proper place in the predicate when it is called.

The percent sign tells **writef** where a format string starts, and we'll see why this is important. The minus sign indicates left justification; if it is left out, the default, right justification, results. Justification here refers to whether the data is printed against the right or left margin of the specified field width.

The optional **m** field specifies the minimum field width. Put **10** here, and nothing else will be written in those 10 spaces. The optional **.p** field operates on both real numbers and strings and tells with what precision you want the variable printed, specifying the precision of a floating point number (the number of decimal places), or the maximum number of characters to be printed out from the string. These must be worked in conjunction with the **m** field to make sure you have allocated enough space to print the called for precision. In using real numbers, you may also use the following three options in place of numbers: an **f** prints in fixed decimal notation, an **e** forces scientific or exponential notation, and a **g** forces the shortest format to be used (this is the default).

There must be a format string for each argument you include in the **writef** predicate. Each of these begins with % and are all combined in **FormatString**. Additionally, you can have regular text. Here's an example:

```
writef("Company Name= %20, Amount Owed= %10.2 \n",
  CompanyName, AmountOwed)
```

This prints out the string **Company Name=**, allocating 20 spaces for it; whatever value is instantiated in the **CompanyName** variable; then does the same for the other variable, allocating only 10 spaces and forcing it (since this is a real number) into dollars and cents representation.

The **\n** at the end of the formatting string is a carriage return. This could be inserted anywhere within the string, making a lengthy form printing predicate easy to design. The other special symbols recognized from within a string are also accepted—such as \t, to cause tabbing.

One other predicate should be mentioned here. You can easily add a provision to access the Turbo Prolog help file in your own programs by making use of the **display** predicate, whose format is **display(String)**.

You may read a text file of up to 64K (around 12,000 words!) into one string variable. Invoking the **display** predicate will display this string variable in the current window, formatting it in a readable manner and allowing the user to page up and down through it with the PgUp, PgDn, and arrow keys.

READING

Seven predicates in Turbo Prolog are important in input of data into your programs. They are **readln, readint, readreal, readchar, inkey, keypressed** (new to version 1.1 of Turbo Prolog), and **file_str**. Like the writing predicates, they can also serve as the basis for more sophisticated reading predicates of your own.

There is one similarity all these reading predicates, with the exception of **file_str**, have in common. They have just one flowpattern, an unbound variable that will find and return a value.

The first of these predefined, standard reading predicates translates as "read a line." Since lines on your computer screen are usually collections of letters and numbers, this is a way to read strings. The format for the predicate is **readln (Line)**, where **Line** is a variable of either string or symbol domain type. This variable must be free—not bound to any value—before its use. The **readln** predicate will accept characters from the read device (usually the keyboard) until a Return is encountered. Limits are 150 characters for a symbol, 64K for a string variable, and up to this limit from other devices such as a modem, another computer or terminal, etc.

Next is **readint(X)**, where X is an integer variable. Again, the variable must be free before the call to the predicate. Characters will be read from the input device until a Return is encountered. The line of characters is then converted into an integer or, if it does not correspond to the usual syntax for integers, the predicate fails and Turbo Prolog's backtracking mechanism is invoked. The limit from −32,766 to 32,767, which means that the maximum number of characters accepted would be five and the value would have to be 32767 or less.

The input predicate for real numbers allows larger and smaller numbers than the integer limit or those having a decimal component to be put into a variable. Its format is **readreal(X)**, where X is a real domain variable. The predicate reads numbers from the input device until a carriage return occurs. The input is then converted into a real number and bound to the variable, assuming that it is in correct syntax for a real

```
                              Help
GRAPHICS
========
dot(Row,Column,Colour)
        (integer,integer,integer) -- (inp,inp,inp) (inp,inp,outp)

graphics(ModeParam,Palette,Background)
        (integer,integer,integer) -- (inp,inp,inp)

line(Row1,Col1,Row2,Col2,Colour)
        (integer,integer,integer,integer,integer)
        -- (inp,inp,inp,inp,inp)

text()


TURTLE GRAPHICS
===============

back(Step)
        (integer) -- (inp)

forward(Step)
        (integer) -- (inp)
```

Fig. 13-2. In addition to the regular dot and line graphics, "turtle" graphics are available through several special predefined predicates.

number—otherwise the predicate fails.

Characters are read by **readchar(CharParam)**, where the variable is a character domain variable. The predicate reads a single character from the input device and binds it to **CharParam**, or whatever you may have named your character variable. The predicate executes as quick as a single character is typed or is entered in some other manner.

Similar in operation, but more rigid, is **inkey(Char)**. This predicate looks for a character on the standard input. If one is present it succeeds, if nothing is there it fails. You can thus use it as an on/off switch in your logic. Like the other read predicates we have met above, it has only the (o) flow pattern, meaning the variable must be free before the predicate is called.

A new predicate added to Turbo Prolog version 1.1 is **keypressed**. This predicate lets you test for a key pressed without reading the character generated by the keystroke into a variable. In operation, **keypressed** succeeds if any key has been pressed; otherwise it fails. As an example of how **keypressed** works, if you insert the predicate **not(keypressed)** into a recursive or some other type of loop, the loop will continue as long as no key is hit, but if a key is pressed, the predicate fails and drops the program out of the loop.

The last input predicate, **file_str(Filename, X)** is the most powerful of all. The domains for the variables **Filename** and **X** must be either symbol or string types. **String** is best as long text slows down operation as symbol table look-up occurs. The variable **X** has to be unbound, and **Filename** is a variable containing an opened for reading MS-DOS file names. When called, **file_str** reads characters from the file until an end-of-file character is encountered. Usually this is a CTRL-Z. The contents of the file are thus transferred to the variable **X**.

One significant feature about using **file_str**, as opposed to **readln**, for example, is that strings generated in this manner can contain carriage returns.

Try this: with two simple steps—**file_str(Manuscript)** and **display(Manuscript)**—you could get a 12,000-word manuscript from a disk file onto your hard disk or floppy in mere seconds, and display it neatly on the screen just as it is formatted in the physical file.

WINDOW COLORS

Windows are those framed areas that pop on and off the screen and make everything look so neat. Turbo Prolog gives you several predicates for manipulating overlapping windows. You can easily open as many as you need, all with optional borders and titles. The actual number depends on how much memory you can spare. Ten is a practical limit (although I've had as many as 15 open at once). You also have complete control of foreground and background colors. It is even possible to change colors character by character, field by field, area by area, giving some really interesting effects.

You can make any particular window the current one and cause the screen input and output to be placed there. Windows can be brought in and out of existence with the greatest of ease. The current window can be changed just as quickly.

Windows allow portions of your computer screens to act independently of other portions. Turbo Prolog lets you have several of these in varying sizes, colors, and functions.

Such windowing ability adds incredible dimension not only to the operation of the programming environment, but also to your own programs. Without windows, only one view, for example of program operation, can be allowed. With windows, you can look at the program listing, the dialog window (in which any results the program obtains are written), a trace window, and any other information that might be beneficial in debugging a piece of software.

An end user of your programs can have an equivalent privilege of displaying a number of independent windows on his or her screen. The text or graphics in each of these scroll without affecting the others. On a color monitor, the interior colors of each are not affected by any of the others. Nor does scrolling and graphics in one window affect what's being displayed in any of the others.

With Turbo Prolog, it is easy to do some very elegant and fancy things with windows and colors. Let's take a little time to determine how colors and other screen attributes are calculated and controlled.

Turbo Prolog allows you to manipulate screen display characteristics, such as inverse video, underlining, and colors. This includes the flex-

```
                                Help
 1. Choose ONE foreground color and ONE background color.
 2. Add the corresponding integer values below.
 3. Add 128 if you want blinking.

BACKGROUND-COLORS (Screen)         FOREGROUND-COLORS (Characters)
-------------------------+----------+---------------+-----------
Black                      0         Black             0
Blue                       16        Blue              1
Green                      32        Green             2
Cyan                       48        Cyan              3
Red                        64        Red               4
Magenta                    80        Magenta           5
Brown                      96        Brown             6
White                      112       White             7
Grey                       8
Light Blue                 24
Light Green                40
Light Red                  72
Light Magenta              88
Yellow                     104
White (High Intensity)     120
```

Fig. 13-3. Color control also is provided in Turbo Prolog.

ibility of having the frame of the window a different color than the interior of the window. Information specifying this manipulation is passed to standard predicates by an attribute value, which then causes the color of the characters (foreground) and the color behind them (background) to be set. You can do this for the whole window or for just one character at a time!

Here's how the display attribute value for a monochrome display adapter is calculated. In doing so you make use of three values: black characters on black background (blank) = 0, white characters on a black background = 7 (normal video which, depending on your monitor, might be green or amber instead), and black characters on a white background (inverse) = 112.

Chose the integer that represents the desired foreground and background combination. Add one if you want the characters to be underlined in the foreground color. Add eight if you want the white (or green or amber) part of the display to be in high intensity. Add 128 if you want the character to blink. Both tables for attribute calculation, monochrome and color, are on page 78 of the *Owner's Handbook*. It's really easy to figure.

Color may look more complex, but it's not. Just the foreground and background attributes: choose the foreground color from the following:

Black	=	0
Blue	=	1
Green	=	2
Cyan	=	3
Red	=	4
Magenta	=	5

Brown	=	6
White	=	7

Now decide on the background, which will become the color of the whole screen or window. These choices are:

Black	=	0
Blue	=	16
Green	=	32
Cyan	=	48
Red	=	64
Magenta	=	80
Brown	=	96
White	=	112
Grey	=	8
Light Blue	=	24
Light Green	=	40
Light Red	=	72
Light Magenta	=	88
Yellow	=	104
Hi-White	=	120

Green has a foreground attribute of 2 and red has a background attribute of 64. If you wanted a screen of green on red you would add the two together and use a screen attribute of 66. If you have a color monitor you will want to experiment to find the most pleasing color combinations for your regular use.

OPENING THE WINDOW

Windows are created with the makewindow predicate. In general format it is:

```
makewindow(WindowNo, ScrAttr, FrameAttr, Header, Row, Column,
   Height, Width)
```

All of these are integers, with the exception of **Header**, which is the optional title of your window and is a string variable. If you do not want a title, simply put a null string (“ ”) in place of **Header**.

In Turbo Prolog version 1.0, there was only one flow pattern attached to this predicate. All variables had to be instantiated, thus it could only be used to create windows. With Turbo Prolog 1.1 the variables may be free, as well. Used in this manner, the **makewindow** predicate will return all the values related to the current window in the appropriate variable.

Time to create a window. Take this as an example:

makewindow(1, 15, 15, "Window On The World," 0, 0, 25, 80).

Remember that it is a clause and must be ended with a period. This particular predicate will cause a window to be created on the screen, which we can then use to perform reading and writing functions.

You will note that the predicate consists of three numbers, a string, and then four more numbers. These are what determine the size and color of the window. The first number inside the parentheses, a one in this case, is the number of the window, giving you a way to jump from window to window if you have more than one on the screen. The second number is the color attribute of the window. We have 15 here, which is bright white on black. Color attributes are exactly the same as you find anywhere in MS-DOS CGA (color graphics adapter) programming. The next number determines the color of the window's frame. We also have it bright white on black.

The string in quotes is the title of the window. Entering " " here will cause no title to appear. The next two numbers specify the starting point of the window, in this case point 0,0—which is the first, top, leftmost point on your screen. The last two designate the size of the window, with 25 lines of 80 columns being the maximum. All these numbers may be replaced with the appropriate domain type variables.

The standard input and output predicates automatically work in the current window. If you create four windows in a row, then cause a string to be written, it appears in the fourth window.

Now let's think about window management for a moment. You can create windows any size you like within the constraints of 25 rows by 80 columns of regular text. Windows can overlap and overlay each other. Provisions are provided to shift between windows while saving the contents of the window you are leaving.

Two easy predicates allow you to do this shifting. The first, **shiftwindow(WindowNo)** will work in any case. It saves the window being left and retrieves the new current window for display. If the new window is large and full of text and especially graphics, this can take discernible time. The second predicate, **gotowindow(WindowNo)** is much faster because it is not buffered. This means that it is useful for switching between windows that do not overly.

The other window control predicates are **clearwindow** and **removewindow** (no arguments for either). They simply blank and close the current window respectively. The example programs numbers 26 (EXAMPL26.PRO), 27 (EXAMPL27), 28 (EXAMPL28) and 29 (EXAMPL29.PRO) on the "Library and Sample Programs" disk are a good introduction to the techniques used in the way Turbo Prolog handles windows. EXAMPL28.PRO is an arcade game and EXAMPL29.PRO is a fun word-guessing game. The latter two also demonstrate some of the special screen-handling predicates that is next up on our agenda.

SCREEN-BASED INPUT AND OUTPUT

The read and write predicates we have talked about so far in this chapter are not adequate for some of the more advanced techniques possible within the graphics and windowing program environment. Other, specially designed and predefined, predicates are provided.

The entire screen or window in a Turbo Prolog program can be accessed and manipulated on three discrete levels: one character at a time, one field at a time (a field is any sequence of character display positions that are contiguous and on the same row), and any one window at a time.

Two predicates are important on the first level, that of one character at a time. These take the forms

```
scr_char(Row, Column, Character)
```

and

```
scr_attr(Row, Column, Attr)
```

The meaning of these are screen character and screen attribute. Attribute is the color determiner (foreground and background) that we just discovered how to calculate.

If the variables **Row**, **Column**, and **Character** are bound in **scr_char**, the letter or number in **Character** will be printed at the position defined by **Row** and **Column**. If this falls outside the window or screen size, an error will be returned. If the character variable is free when the predicate is invoked, the character at the designated row and column position will be returned. And **scr_attr** does exactly the same for the attribute of the position.

On the fields level we have two equivalent predicates, except that these have an extra variable added to specify the length of the field. Fields can be any size from 2 characters wide to 80 wide. In general form these predicates are

```
field_str(Row, Column, Length, String)
```

and

```
field_attr(Row, Column, Length, Attr)
```

```
|     Run      Compile     Edit      Options      Files      Setup      Quit     |

------------------------------------- Editor -----------------------------------
|  Line 1      Col 1      Indent   Insert  EXAMPL39.PRO                          |
|/* Program 39 */                                                               |
|/*                                                                             |
|  NOTE:  all graphics programs are in white on a                               |
|  black(blue) background. If you don't like this                               |
|  combination it can easily be changed.  You                                   |
|  can change the parameters to the 'graphics'                                  |
|  predicate, or you can  change the drawing                                    |
|  color. Read page 92 and try some combinations                                |
|  of parameters.  For example: graphics(1,5,17)                                |
|  on a CGA will give you pink  letters and a                                   |
|  white line on a blue background. Other systems                               |
|  give  different colors. Just explore.                                        |
|*/                                                                             |
|                                                                               |
|predicates                                                                     |
|  circle(real)                                                                 |
|                                                                               |
|goal                                                                           |

Use first letter of option  or  select with  ->  or  <-
```

Fig. 13-4. Example program 39 demonstrates graphics.

Field_str works like **scr_char** does, and can be used to read or write text to a field on the screen or inside a window. The location of the field is specified by the variables **Row** and **Column** and **Length**, all of which must define a field that can fit on the screen or, if windows are present, within the window to which it is addressed. If **String** is bound to a value longer than **Length** indicates, only **Length** number of characters will be printed and the rest are chopped off. If **String** is shorter than **Length**, the remainder of the field will be filled with blank spaces. All the positions in a particular field can be assigned an attribute by one call of the **field_attr** predicate.

The predicate **window_str(StringParam)** is more flexible and more powerful than the character and field writing predicates we've just met. If **StringParam** is free when **window_str** is called, it will be bound to the string currently being displayed in the window and have the same number of lines. If it is already bound to a value, that string will be written. The length of every line in the string is determined by the last non-blank character in the line.

Here's where the real difference comes in—the previous two levels' predicates are restricted to positions actually on just one row, existing within the boundaries of the screen or window. If **StringParam** in **window_str** is bound to a value, however, it will be written in the window according to these criteria: If there are more lines in the string than lines in the window, lines will be written until all the window space is used up. If there are fewer lines in the string than in the window, the remaining lines will be filled with blank spaces. If there are more characters in a string line than are available on a window line, the string line is truncated to fit. If there are fewer characters in a line than there are columns in the window, the line will be filled with blank space.

The predicates that control colors or other attributes on this level are **attribute(Attr)** and **window_attr(Attr)**. The operation of these are a bit ambiguous, since both will work within a window. Remember that *screen* refers to the entire computer screen, but that there can be several windows or portions of the screen that are independent in color to each other.

The slick windowing and color/attribute control offered by Turbo Prolog make the design and implementation of attractive professional program a snap.

GRAPHICS

In addition to windowing, Turbo Prolog handles the standard IBM PC and compatible graphics modes and several of the EGA (Enhanced Graphics Adapter) modes, as well as various sound effects. Predefined predicates are available that will plot points, draw lines, and perform turtle graphics. Turbo Prolog's graphics modes work in conjunction with the windows, also. Over all, there are around 30 predicates for text and graphics screen-related operations. you will find these indexed beginning on page 180 of the Turbo Prolog *Owners Handbook*.

As far as colors and resolution go, you have several choices available. These include 320 columns × 200 rows CGA medium resolution in four colors (CGA is the IBM standard Colors/Graphics adapter), 640 columns × 200 rows CGA high resolution black and white, 320 × 200 EGA medium resolution in 16 colors, 640 × 200 EGA high resolution in 16 colors, and 640 × 350 EGA enhanced resolution in 13 colors. The appropriate color adapter cards and color monitors must be in place to access these.

Before any of the Turbo Prolog graphics predicates are called, you must first set up the screen for their operation. This is done with the standard predicate

```
graphics(ModeParam, Palette, Background)
```

Once the graphics portion of the program is done, the screen is returned to normal text mode with the predicate **text**, which has no arguments.

Why is this change necessary? The way IBM PC's work in text mode is this. If an A needs to be printed, there is a device called a character generator that tells the computer what an A looks like. Since this character is already formed and in memory, it can be written to the screen ex-

```
      Run      Compile      Edit      Options      Files      Setup      Quit

------------------------------------ Editor ------------------------------------
  Line 1      Col 1      Indent  Insert  EXAMPL40.PRO
/* Program 40 */

domains
    list=integer*

predicates
    spotlight(integer,integer,integer)
    xy(list)
    undo

goal
    graphics(2,0,1),
    makewindow(1,7,7,"First",1,1,18,70),
    xy(°0,0,0,6000,4000,20500,20000,24000,16100,1000§),
    xy(°0,0,0,9000,3000,26500,20100,24400,20100,1000§),
    makewindow(2,7,7,"Second",10,20,14,60),
    xy(°0,1000,0,9000,0,20000,15000,20000,15000,1000§),
    makewindow(3,7,7,"Text",15,0,6,35),

Use first letter of option  or  select with  ->  or  <-
```

Fig. 13-5. This spotlight effect requires a graphics board; run example program 40.

ceptionally fast. In text mode, there is room for a maximum number of 25 rows times 80 columns, or 2000 positions. This is nothing for a computer, so screen writing in text mode is fast.

Printing an A, drawing a line, or anything else in graphics mode is quite different. Here the screen is divided into much smaller positions. In the standard CGA medium resolution of 320 × 200, we are talking about 64,000 positions. If you have an EGA card installed in your computer, it becomes 640 × 350 or 224,000 positions! Even at computer speed, it takes time to punch in all these tiny little dots.

So, there is a trade-off between better appearance and display write time when you are using graphics. You have to decide on whether or not each instance is worth it.

The screen is initialized to graphics with the predicate

```
graphics(ModeParam, Palette, Background)
```

The variable **ModeParam** refers to the five modes currently supported by Turbo Prolog and listed on page 92 of the *Owner's Handbook*. The values for **Palette** and **Background** are also on the same page. As in setting screen attributes, you will want to experiment with these three to find the most pleasing or striking combinations.

In discussing screen position, we've talked about the 25 rows × 80 columns of text mode and the 320 × 200, 640 × 200, and 640 × 320 positions of CGA and EGA color cards. Turbo Prolog has a third way of addressing actual dot position on graphics screens. In this method, both **Row** and **Column** are integers from zero to 31999 *regardless* of the graphics resolution mode selected in the graphics predicate. This means that point 0,0 is the extreme upper left corner of the screen, and 31999,31999 is the bottom-most right-hand position, and 16000,16000 is very close to the exact center. An IBM or compatible system currently cannot actually address all those points.

The basic reference point is called a *dot*. The **dot(Row, Column, Color)** predicate can be used in two ways. The first puts a dot of specific color at that position; the second (unbound) returns whatever color attribute exists at the exact point indicated by **Row** and **Column**. Some experimenting to get the field of the zero to 31999 range of both **Row** and **Column** will be necessary.

To speed things up in line drawing, a predefined standard line predicate is supplied. This is:

```
line(Row1, Column1, Row2, Col2, Color)
```

where the points for the start and end of the line are specified and the color selected. Example program numbers 34 (EXAMPL34.PRO), 35 (EXAMPL35.PRO), 36 (EXAMPL36.PRO), 37 (EXAMPLE.37), 38 (EXAMPLE38), 39 (EXAMPL39), and 40 (EXAMPL40.PRO) on the "Library and Sample Programs" disk are a good introduction to the methods used in Turbo Prolog manipulation of graphics.

Then there is our friend the turtle—star of turtle graphics! The turtle, as described by the *Owner's Handbook* and as it is used in other implementations of Prolog, LISP, and various other languages, is a little cursor that, when the graphics screen is initialized, appears in the middle of the screen with its head pointed to the top and its tail to the bottom. The tail of the turtle is grasping a "pen." The turtle will move under your direction, turning this way and that, dragging the pen whenever you want it to draw a line in whatever color may be desired.

The idea was developed to educate young children and the name stuck. What's more, the turtle in Turbo Prolog, like the 6-foot rabbit in *Harvey*, is invisible. And not only is it invisible, it is imaginary to boot.

Several predicates control the turtle's travels, when it drags its pen, and in what color the line is laid down on the screen. The predicates **pendown** and **penup** (both require no arguments) cause the turtle to put the pen down in writing position and to pull it back up. The color of the trail left by a down pen is specified by **pencolor(Color)**. Color is determined as for foreground colors, so Color = 1 would draw a blue line and Color = 2 a green one.

Turtle movement is controlled with four predicates: **forward(Step)**,

back(Step), **right(Angle)**, and **left(Angle)**. The variable **Step** contains the number of units for the turtle to move, and 31999 would move it all the way across the screen from top to bottom or from left to right (with Turbo Prolog automatically adjusting for the fact that computer screens are rectangular).

The variable **Angle** used in the **right** and **left** predicates causes the turtle to rotate the number of angle degrees that you specify, from 1 to 36. If you want to draw a circle, you can construct a circle predicate like this clause:

```
circle:-forward(1000), right(1), circle
```

which will cause the turtle to go around in circles on a graphics screen. This is Program 39, by the way, on page 95 of the *Owners Handbook*. Try it, it's neat.

THE SOUND OF MUSIC

To go along with the pretty pictures, Turbo Prolog can make your computer do sound effects or even play tunes. Two simple predicates control all this. The first takes the form **beep**, and has no arguments. All it does is make your computer beep. The second, **sound(Duration, Frequency)** is more powerful.

In operating this latter predicate, a note of **Frequency** is played for **Duration** hundredths of a second. Musical notes, of course, are of known frequencies. Low C is 131 cycles per second (now called Hertz), D is 147, E is 165, F is 175, G is 196, A is 220, B is 247, middle C is 262, and so on.

Example program numbers 41 (EXAMPL41.PRO), and 42 (EXAMPL42.PRO) on the "Library and Sample Programs" disk demonstrate sound, with 42 being a rudimentary emulation of a piano using your computer's keyboard. If you are musically inclined, this would be fun to elaborate into a greater range and more voices.

Chapter 14

Databases, Expert Systems, Natural Language

SINCE TURBO PROLOG REPRESENTS A RELATIONAL DATABASE AS A collection of facts, you can easily create programs that act as a powerful query language. The internal workings of Prolog's logic structure, especially its unification algorithm, automatically selects facts that have the correct values for the known parameters and will assign values to unknown ones, backtracking to collect all possible solutions.

These collections of facts are called *dynamic* databases. Because of the need to increase speed while working with large databases, facts belonging to dynamic databases in Turbo Prolog are handled differently from regular facts and relationships. Dynamic database predicates are even declared in their own section, **database**, instead of the **domains** section.

DECLARATION AND MANIPULATION

The database declarations section of a Turbo Prolog program, like the other sections, is defined simply by placing that keyword against the left-hand margin. You can then follow the keyword with a series of predicate declarations for predicates which describe a dynamic database.

The term *dynamic* here refers to a database in which facts may be added during execution of the program, or may be pulled from a disk file. The database declarations must take place before the regular predicates are declared. A sample declaration is:

person(name, address, age, sex)

where name and address have previously been declared in the domains section as strings. **Age** is an integer and **sex** is a symbol with one of two meanings designated by the domains declaration **sex** = **male; female.** Again, the semicolon means **or**.

The **person** database predicate can be used exactly like you would use any other predicate. The major difference is that it is possible to insert and remove facts from this predicate during operation of the program.

Turbo Prolog has three standard, predefined predicates for database manipulation. These are **asserta(fact)**, **assertz(fact)**, and **retract(fact)**. All **facts** can be strings or symbols. The first predicate inserts a new fact before any others already in memory for that particular database relation; the second puts the new fact after all the others (use the last letters, a and z, to help you remember that). The last predicate removes a fact from the database collection. A fact is modified by first retracting it, then reinserting the changed fact with either asserta or assertz.

The entire database is saved to disk by using the predicate **save(Filename)**, with the name of a text file as its argument. If you look into the resulting file on the disk it will resemble an ordinary Turbo Prolog program file with a fact on each line. Database files on disk are read back into memory by using the **consult(Filename)** predicate. The **consult** predicate succeeds if the file has no format errors, otherwise it fails.

```
                                    Help

SPECIAL - PREDICATES
====================
asserta( Term )
assertz( Term )
bound( Variable )
findall( Variable, Atom, ListVariable )
free( Variable )
not( Atom )
readterm( Domain, Variable )
retract( Term )
write( VariableùConstant * )
writef( FormatString, VariableùConstant * )


              OPTIONS

```

Fig. 14-1. The special predicates that make powerful database manipulation possible.

A predicate useful for bringing information into the database from outside is **readterm(Term)**. **Term** can be a compound object such as

```
readterm(member (FirstName, MI, LastName, AddressLine1,
   AddressLine2, City, State, ZIP, DuesOwed, Comments
```

where each variable has been appropriately typed and declared in the domains section. The **readterm** predicate can read anything that has been written by a corresponding **write(compound_object)**.

Such facts as those that describe database predicates can also be manipulated as if they were actually terms. This is because of a special predefined **dbasedom** domain. It is automatically predeclared by Turbo Prolog, and provides one alternative for each predicate in the database. Each database predicate is described by a functor and by the domains of the arguments (symbols and variables) in that predicate.

For example, if you were to declare a database as **person(name, telephone)** and **city(address, city)**, Turbo Prolog would automatically generate a domain equivalent to:

```
dbasedom = person(name, telephone) ; city(address, city)
```

This domain can be used just like any other predefined domain.

As you master the basics of database manipulation in Turbo Prolog, you will want to extend your techniques to include maintaining and manipulating large databases while still in their various files, instead of loading them into memory first. A hint of the techniques you will need to master start on page 142 of the Turbo Prolog *Owner's Manual.*

Database facts are part of Turbo Prolog programs; without file manipulation you are limited to the amount of your working memory, minus the amount taken up by MS-DOS, minus any memory-resident utilities. You also have to subtract that part of the Prolog program that is not database facts. But with file manipulation you are limited only to the size of your floppies and/or hard drives.

EXPERT SYSTEMS

One of the two major artificial intelligence applications for which Turbo Prolog is especially well suited is expert systems. The other is natural language interfacing. Both make heavy use of database manipulation techniques, and both are easy to construct and use.

Questions in expert systems are phrased in plain English and are questions we would ask of experts like doctors, geologists, industrial engineers, and so on, such as: "This man has a fever and is perspiring heavily, what is wrong with him?" "There are traces of blue clay on this property, what minerals should I look for?"

Human experts are not always around when you need them; computers usually are. A human expert, given the proper software, can answer a series of questions, the software can store them, and when you ask the program questions it will answer as if the expert him or herself were there.

The "fuzzy" part of this is accomplished by weighting the expert's opinions. He or she may be 60 percent certain that if certain facts are present, a specific result has a better than average chance of occurring. By asking and obtaining answers to a series of related questions you have an even greater percentage of certainty. This is what an expert system does.

One of the classic demonstrations of artificial intelligence expert systems is a guessing game named "Animals." "Animals" asks you questions, and learns from your answers. The game works like this: you think of an animal and the program tries to guess it.

Example program number 51 (EXAMPL51.PRO) on the "Library and Sample Programs" disk is an implementation of this very game! It's used as a demonstration in how a small expert system can be constructed. A more sophisticated expert system is given with Turbo Prolog version 1.1 and higher, called GENI, found in the PROGRAMS subdirectory.

Load EXAMPL51. This program figures out which of the seven animals in its database (if any) you have in mind. A sample dialog might go something like this:

Program: Has it hair?
You: Yes.
Program: Does it eat meat?
You: Yes.
Program: Has it a fawn color?
You: Yes.
Program: Has it dark spots?
You: Yes.
Program: Your animal may be a (an) cheetah!

Using this program as an example will show you how the facts and rules that are necessary to build an expert system are easily handled in Turbo Prolog.

NATURAL LANGUAGE

Natural language recognition is the ability of a program to accept and successfully understand common, everyday sentences. Turbo Prolog is quite adept at natural language interfacing.

Two important examples of natural language "parsing" are supplied with your Turbo Prolog package. The first is in the PROGRAMS subdirectory on the "Library and Sample Programs" disk. It's called SANAL and is a sentence analyzer. Remember how your high-school English teacher used to make you diagram sentences? This program does it for you! It's a very good guide to the type of predicates and techniques you need in natural language recognition and processing.

The extensive Geobase intelligent database that you will find on the Program Disk can be run either from within the programming environment, or compiled and used as a standard stand-alone program. It is intended as a wealth of example techniques to be used in your own artificial intelligence applications.

Geobase demonstrates a natural language interface to a database on U.S. geography. The database contains data about the United States in various categories. There is information on Geobase extracted from the GEOBASE.HLP file supplied on the Program disk of your Turbo Prolog package.

You can retrieve any or all of the information in Geobase by asking questions in normal English. Some sample queries are: "Give me the cities in california"; "what is the longest river in the usa?"; "what is the name of the state with the lowest point?"; and so on.

You can modify Geobase as you work with it. If it doesn't understand a word in one of your questions, you can add the word to the language definition. The language is defined in a number of relations, the most important being the schema. A *schema* is a description of the logical structure of a database. In Geobase, the schema is the "entity network" for the language. A schema entry follows the form:

```
entity association entity;
```

This signifies that the two entities are bound together by the given association.

This program is very sophisticated and chock full of predicates you need for your own programming library. It is provided precisely for this purpose. The program files are heavily commented to help you decipher and extract predicates and techniques. For the actual parser predicates, look from line 220 of this file down.

Chapter 15

Advanced Programming Techniques

TURBO PROLOG HAS SEVERAL FEATURES THAT LET YOU WRITE and implement programs much more complicated than the ones we have covered so far. Many of these advanced and/or specialized predicates interact with each other, so I will group them together here in somewhat of a catch-all manner.

Our purpose here is to shed some light on the more advanced subjects covered in the "Programmer's Guide" of the Turbo Prolog *Owner's Handbook*. As such (like all of this book), the material here should be used to supplement not replace that in the *Handbook*. And even so, both of them are only a starting point in learning Prolog. Once you get the basics of terminology and the mechanics of declarative programming under your belt, then you can move on to and understand more advanced texts.

MEMORY MANAGEMENT

As far as the Turbo Prolog system is concerned, the available working memory in your computer is divided into five parts. These are called Stack, Heap, Trail, Code, and Source. Let's look at Source, since it affects the amount of memory available to Turbo Prolog. The source area is for text, the program listing. This area may be increased by using "include" files.

Turbo Prolog puts the compiled program in Code. In a very large program, if there is not enough memory allocated to receive the code, the process will bomb out and compiling will abort. The default size for code is 16 kilobytes, or exactly 16,384 characters of storage.

If more space for code is needed, this is set by the **code** directive, entered just as you would a **domains, predicates**, or **clauses** keyword. The format to use is **code = Number_of_paragraphs**, where **Number_of_paragraphs** is the number of 16-byte memory paragraphs required in the code array. You can decrease code size if more space is needed for stack, or one of the other memory areas.

The Trail area registers the binding and unbinding of reference variables, but is not normally needed in Turbo Prolog hence its default size is zero. If you do want to use a trail, you can specify the area be created with the **trail = Number_of_Words** compiler directive (used in the same manner as the one for changing Code area). For most purposes, **trail = 100** will be more than sufficient.

Skipping **Heap** for the moment, we come to the head of the list, Stack. Stack is used for parameter transfer, especially in programs where tail recursion occurs. It works in the manner of a snake eating its own tail, regenerating and doing it again and again. Such a process can easily get out of control, soaking up memory and time to the detriment of efficiency, so tools such as the **cut** predicate are used to put the snake on a diet, where necessary.

To allow greater recursion in programs where tail recursion cannot be controlled, the stack size can be increased. This is done within the programming environment of Turbo Prolog. Choose Settings from the main menu bar, then the Miscellaneous option. On the resulting submenu is the Stack size option. The default value is 600 paragraphs, or 9600 bytes. Any value between 9600 bytes, up to and including the maximum of 4000 paragraphs (64K) is permissible. This set-up must be saved and reloaded to put the change into effect.

Once the Stack, Source, Code, and Trail (if there is one) areas are allocated, any remaining memory is used for the Heap. The Heap is used for two different purposes. Within the Heap itself, a stack (not to be confused with **Stack**) is used by Turbo Prolog to build structures, store strings, and so forth, during program operation. When a particular predicate fails, this space is released. Facts being inserted into a database also reside in the Heap. Memory area is automatically released whenever possible to keep Heap demands as low as possible.

If you want a test to get an idea of the memory overhead being soaked up by your program, this standard predefined predicate:

```
storage(StackSize, HeapSize, TrailSize)
```

will return the available size of Stack, Heap, and Trail respectively. If memory use is a problem, you can fiddle with the logical operation of your program to reduce one area in order to make necessary space in another.

COMPILER CONTROL

Running your programs from within the programming environment is neat and a great way to iron out the kinks, but the real fun is in creating stand-alone programs you can give to your friends, up-load to electronic bulletin boards, or sell to clients. This is done by compiling your program text files into executable machine code, a process accomplished automatically by Turbo Prolog via the Compile selection on the main menu bar within the constraints you have imposed on it. The Options submenu (Fig. 15-1) is one of the ways in which you control compiling.

The default option is the one you will use the most during development phases. This compiles the program within your working memory and gives you immediate operation. The program is stored there until you compile another or exit Turbo Prolog. You can run the program over and over without having to go through the sometimes moderately lengthy compilation process each time. It's much like using a BASIC interpreter in this respect. You get interaction during programming, and can try out a number of things until you find the best mode of operation. Only then do you compile a finished result to disk. The following choices in the Options submenu concern that.

The "OBJ file" option places your program in a binary file but does not link it (set it up to be run independently). You can exit to your operating system and use an external linker like the one supplied with MS-DOS or PC-DOS. Turbo Prolog might not have room to compile the program while it is resident itself in your computer's working memory.

The "EXE (auto link)" option causes your program to be compiled

```
                                  Help

                    OPTIONS

trace              traces all predicates.
trace p1,p2,..     trace predicates p1,p2,... only.
shorttrace         tracing without disturbing system optimizing. (Ref. p11.4.9)
nowarnings         Suppress warnings from variable used only once
nobreak            Predicates should not scan the keyboard to see
                   if CTRL-BREAK has been pressed.
check_determ       This directive instructs the compiler to give a warning
                   about the presence of a nondeterministic clause.
                   In combination with this directive, the programmer has
                   the option to explicitly describe which state of
```

Fig. 15-1. Options that allow the user to trace or otherwise structure Turbo Prolog programs.

into a stand-alone program when Compile is chosen from the main menu bar. Version 1.0 uses DOS .BAT files to invoke Microsoft's linker (LINK.EXE)—make sure LINK.EXE (version 2.14 or greater) is present or in a DOS path where it can be found by the compiling process. Version 1.1 has its own built-in linker, which has the added benefit of generating slightly smaller EXE (executable) programs.

The last option, "PROJECT (all modules)," has been added to Version 1.1 and allows programs to be written in small, easier-to-understand chunks which can be joined together during compilation. You may also develop and use a series of standard modules, speeding up development time.

It is possible to automatically compile all modules in a project. Select Compile Project under the Options pull-down menu, give the name of the project, select the Compile option, and all the modules will be compiled. The Prolog modules should reside in the PRO directory, and the .PRJ file should reside on the .OBJ directory.

COMPILER DIRECTIVES

Another important way of controlling the compiling process is by the use of embedded keywords in the text of your Turbo Prolog program text files. Two of these directives, **code** and **trail**, we've already met; the full list available in Version 1.1 of Turbo Prolog is **check_cmpio**, **check_determ**, **code**, **diagnostics**, **include**, **nobreak**, **nowarnings**, **project**, **shorttrace** and **trace**, and **trail**. These are entered as keywords, and you can have more than one of them, as needed.

Whenever the **check_cmpio** directive is specified, you will receive a warning if compound flow patterns are used. This means that if a predicate is called in which some subcomponents are bound and others are not, such as one that takes a specific name in a membership list and returns address, city, state, etc. Nothing wrong with this if the logic of your program calls for it, but such a mixture in compound flow patterns generate more code. Thus this directive is a tool you can use to understand the operation of your programs. If compound flow patterns exist that are not needed, this will point them out and you can take steps to tone up program operation.

The next directive, **check_determ**, gives a warning for each nondeterministic predicate. Remember the **cut** predicate? Let's take an example. If you had the New York City telephone directory on your hard disk as a data file and wanted to know what was the first name beginning with S, Turbo Prolog's relentless backtracking would result in all people whose name starts with an 'S' being listed. The predicate doing this is termed nondeterministic, getting every solution it can find.

By placing a **cut** operator before the variable being used to return names starting with S, we can make it deterministic—once the first solution is found, the search for solutions is cut off. So, using the **check_determin** compiler directive will tell you which predicates are nondeterministic. Thus, in a long program, you can put **cut** operators in front of the predicates that do not need to be nondeterministic, speeding up program operation and saving memory space.

During the compilation process the **diagnostics** keyword will cause an analysis of your program to be displayed. The information shown includes the name of predicates used, whether or not all the clauses for these predicates are facts, indicates if the predicate is deterministic or nondeterministic, lists the size of code for each predicate, indicates the flow patterns, and shows the domain types of the parameters. This directive is extremely handy in debugging your own programs or understanding someone else's.

The **include** keyword is used to include another program text file in a program during compilation. The most important use of this is to easily include subprograms out of your library, such as menus and so on. The format for including another program file is **include "dos-file-name"**.

Such included files may only be used on *natural* boundaries of programs. This means that the keyword **include** (along with the name of the appropriate MS-DOS file) may only appear where one of the keywords—**domains, predicates, clauses**, or **goal**—is permitted. Include files may contain calls to other include files, which may in turn contain nested include files. These files may contain a goal or domains and predicates declarations, as needed.

The **nowarnings** directive suppresses the warnings normally given by Turbo Prolog when a variable occurs only once in a clause or is not bound on return from the clause. There are instances, such as dummy variables, when you really don't care what the variable does, but use it as a place marker.

Project is used in modular programming and takes the form **project "MYPROJ"**. We will explore modular programming later in this chapter.

The allied directives **trace** and **shorttrace** may be inserted in your programs for use during the debugging process. The difference between them is that **trace** prevents Turbo Prolog from carrying out the elimination of tail recursion and the various other optimizing tricks employed. Thus, all calls and returns are shown in the trace window. The **shorttrace** option steps through the program with all these optimizations recognized and used.

If either of these two keywords are present, all predicates will be traced. If a list of predicates follow **trace** or **shorttrace** *only* those predicates will be traced. This is a nice feature used for debugging very large programs, allowing you to narrow problem areas until they are found.

Regardless of the keyword used in tracing, one of four results is displayed in the trace window. CALL displays the called predicate's name and the values of its parameters. RETURN is displayed in the trace window when a clause is satisfied and the predicate returns to any calling predicate. If there are additional clauses that match the parameters, an asterisk will be displayed to indicate the clause is at a backtracking point.

FAIL is shown in the trace window to let you know that a predicate failed in resolving its attempted operation. The name of the predicate appears after it. REDO shows that backtracking has taken place. The name of the predicate being retried and the values of its parameters are shown. The use of these powerful trace features make debugging a breeze.

The last compiler directive, **trail**, was discussed earlier.

MODULAR PROGRAMMING

Even a car factory doesn't put together a whole car from scratch; they use *subassemblies*. This is the same technique that almost all professional programmers use, tying a lot of small modules together. You need to develop a library of these; then, when a program is needed, you can plop in a menu, a sorter, and so on. Modules can be written, edited, and even compiled separately, and then linked together to make a single executable program. In this manner you can take advantage of the fact that, in the default configuration, all predicates and domain names are localized to the particular module, meaning that you can use a particular name different ways in various parts of the program, as appropriate.

Turbo Prolog offers two major features in modular programming that are important—*projects* and *global declarations*. These, among other things, let you maintain a record of which modules make up a program (called a project), and perform type-checking across module boundaries.

When you want to combine separate modules into a program, Turbo Prolog requires that you supply a *project definition* which tells it the names of the modules involved. You must create a file called the LIBRARIAN which contains this list of module names. The contents of this file take the form (one per line) of: **name_of_first_module+**, **name_of_second_module+**, and so forth.

Each module is designated by its first name only, which means no file type, and is followed by a plus sign. The file name of the project definition file becomes the name for the whole project, and must have a file extension .PRJ.

So, the first step in modular programming is to think of a name for your project, then to create the project definition file. This is done with the Module List option, found on the Files pull-down submenu. When you are asked for a name, name your project. You will then be deposited within the editor window. Note that Turbo Prolog has automatically given your file name a .PRJ extension. Enter your module names, one per line, terminating each line with +. You can edit these project lists as many times as you like, using the same procedure, via the Files Module List option.

GLOBAL DOMAINS AND PREDICATES

Moving on to the second part of modular programming, global declarations: The default situation in projects is that all the names used in a particular module are local; they have no effect on the same names in another module. You *are* allowed to have predicates that communicate across module boundaries. These special predicates must be declared in a "global predicates" section, and the domains used in them must be defined as global domains, or else be of a standard type. The word "global" means that it is the same in all the modules of the project.

A domain is made global by writing it in a global domains program section. In all other respects, it is exactly the same ordinary local domain declarations. Global predicate declarations, however, have a major difference from their purely local counterparts. They must also contain a description of the flow pattern or patterns in which each given predicate may be called. This must follow this scheme:

```
mypred(d1, d2, ... , dan) - (f,f, ... ,f) (f, f, ... , f) ... ,
```

where d1, d2, etc. are global domains and each group (f, f, . . ., f) denotes a flow pattern in which f is either i (input or instantiated parameter) or o (an output parameter). If any global definition is changed, then *all* modules in that project need to be recompiled.

Additional information on modular programming starts on page 152 of the *Owner's Handbook*. A sample project with global declarations is MAIN.PRO, which is in the EXAMPLES subdirectory on the "Library & Sample Programs" disk.

INTERFACING WITH OTHER LANGUAGES

If Turbo Prolog is so great, why bother with any other languages? While Prolog is an excellent tool for many applications, it's easier to perform numeric integration in Fortran; interrupt handling is done better in assembly language; and if you are one of the hundreds of thousands who have been using Pascal, there is no need to rewrite lengthy procedures you already have worked out. At the present time Turbo Prolog supports Pascal, C, Fortran, and assembler.

The calling conventions to inform Turbo Prolog that a global predicate is implemented in another language are reasonably simple. A language specification is attached to the global predicate declaration. For example:

```
add(integer, integer, integer) – (i, i, o), (i, i, i) language C
```

or

```
scanner(string, token) – (i, o) language Pascal
```

Examples of calls to assembler, C, Pascal, and Fortran routines are given in the *Owner's Handbook*, starting on page 156.

PROCEDURAL TECHNIQUES

One horse we have ridden hard throughout this book is the advantages of declarative over procedural languages. And it is true that essentially everything which can be done in C or Pascal or BASIC also can be done in Turbo Prolog. Yet, this doesn't mean that procedural techniques from these older languages readily become pure declarative ones.

It is sometimes more advantageous to program *procedurally* in Turbo Prolog. Dr. Michael A. Covington of the University of Georgia's Advanced Computational Methods Center has written a very helpful paper on this entitled "Expressing Procedural Algorithms in Prolog," in which the examples are in Turbo Prolog syntax. The paper is available for just the connect time while down-loading from several of the national computer networks. The file is well worth having and reading for any serious programmer.

On Delphi—the international network of General Videotex headquartered in Cambridge, Massachusetts—the paper can be found in the Programming section of the MS-DOS Special Interest Group database. After entering the SIG, this is accessed by typing "DA PR", then "DIR" to get a directory of the file. On-line help is available for down-loading to your computer. (See Appendix B for Delphi sign-up information.)

The paper is 3652 words long which, at 1200 baud, takes less than 6 minutes to pull into your computer. Covington also has written a very nice programmer's editor program (called the Ad Hoc Editor) which is available in the same database; it will edit lines in excess of 30,000 characters and works rather elegantly.

Dr. Covington has kindly granted permission for us to take an overview look at what is contained in the paper.

Here is Dr. Covington's description of his paper: "With the increasing popularity of Prolog as an application programming language, it is often necessary to develop Prolog equivalents for algorithms that were originally expressed in procedure-oriented languages. This paper presents a number of strategies for doing so. I assume that the reader is already familiar with the basic mechanisms of Prolog—unification (matching), backtracking, and the like."

And one more quote, this to define this procedural interpretation of logic: "Prolog is often described as a nonprocedural language. In reality, it is a semi-procedural language—a compromise between procedural and nonprocedural programming, giving some of the advantages of each. In a truly nonprocedural language, the programmer would provide only a logically rigorous set of conditions that the program must fulfill; the computer would then automatically generate an algorithm from them. Such things as the order in which the conditions were written would have no effect.

"In the interest of efficiency, Prolog contains some procedural elements. The Prolog programmer specifies not only the rules of inference to be used in solving a problem, but also the order in which they are to be tried. Crucially, the programmer can even specify that some potential paths to a solution should not be tried at all. This makes it possible to perform efficiently many computations that would be severely inefficient, or even impossible, in pure Prolog."

In BASIC and the other procedural languages, there are two fundamental techniques used in programming: *branching* and *looping*. Almost every program written contains variants of one or both of these techniques (Figs. 15-2, 15-3, and 15-4). Dr. Covington's paper explores

```
        /* a loop in Turbo Prolog that will
           write numbers to the screen until
           any key is pressed (this uses the
           new "keypressed" predicate)      */

domains
        n = real
predicates
        test(n)
goal
        clearwindow,
        makewindow(1,14,2,"loop test in Turbo Prolog",0,0,25,80),
        test(1),
        removewindow,
        clearwindow.

clauses
        test(N):-
                not(keypressed),
                write(N," "),
                M = N+1 and M <> 100,!,
                test(M).
```

Fig. 15-2. A program loop in Turbo Prolog.

```
          /* a loop with conditional exit */

domains
        n = integer

predicates
        writeTest100Times(n)
        repeat
goal
        writeTest100Times(100).

clauses
        repeat.
        repeat:-repeat.
        writeTest100Times(N):-
                NN=101-N,
                write(NN," Test "),nl,
                M=N-1,
                not(M=0),
                writeTest100Times(M).
```

Fig. 15-3. A Turbo Prolog loop with a conditional exit.

both of these as they relate to Prolog.

Conditional execution in Turbo Prolog, unlike pure branching in other languages, is implemented *not* with if or case conditions, but with alternative definitions. If you want a predicate to do three different opera-

```
        /* the rudiments of conditional
           branching in Turbo Prolog */


domains
        num = integer

predicates
        writename(num)

clauses
        writename(1):-!,write("One"),nl.
        writename(2):-!,write("Two"),nl.
        writename(3):-!,write("Three"),nl.
        writename(_):-!,write("Out of range"),nl.
```

Fig. 15-4. Conditional branching is possible in Turbo Prolog.

tions under three different conditions, you would give it as many definitions.

Thus, in the technique shown in Michael Covington's paper, if you wanted to define a predicate such as this:

```
writename(integerVariable)
```

to write the name of the correct integer, you would have matching clauses such as:

```
writename(1):-!, write("One").
```

and

```
writename(2):-!, write("Two").
```

When the variable is 1, "One" is written; or 2 clauses "Two" to be written. The cut operators are in the clauses to ensure that only *one* solution for each condition is found. You can easily expand on this technique for all your procedural conditional branching needs.

There are two ways to perform loops in Turbo Prolog, either through backtracking or recursion. For a repeat-fail loop, in which the loop continues until a certain condition is met, backtracking works but is not the best. One way to achieve a loop in Turbo Prolog is to define a **repeat** predicate. Then, in the clauses section, add the two clauses, **repeat**. and **repeat:- repeat**.. Now if you were to give this goal:

```
repeat, write ("test "), fail,
```

the loop writing "test " will do so until you interrupt it, since **repeat** never fails on its own.

The way this loop works is that **fail** forces it to backtrack and try another solution every time it's encountered. If, however, instead of **fail** as the last predicate, we use something that lets it eventually succeed, the looping will be ended.

This is not always easy since, unlike in BASIC or Pascal, the variables do not retain their value when backtracking occurs. But Dr. Covington suggests an easy way to do it via recursion, which I have modified very slightly. You can experiment and come up with conditional looping techniques for your various applications.

To write the word "Test" 100 times, I did it like this. Two predicates are declared, the **repeat** predicate as above, and one named **writeTest100Times(n)**. The necessary two repeat clauses are put in the clauses section, then the clause that does all the work is inserted. This is:

```
writeTest100Times(N):– NN=100–N, write(NN, Test "),n1,
   M=N–1, not(M=0), writeTest100Times(M).
```

This will write 100 lines, numbering them "1 Test," "2 Test," "3 Test," etc.

Here's how the loop works. The goal **writeTest100Times(100)** is given. The clause is called with N = 100. NN is generated from N merely to serve as an ascending rather than descending count to be written out. So, 101 - 100 means that the write predicate causes "1 Test" to be written to your computer screen. M = N-1 or 99; 99 is not equal to zero, so the clause is called again, only this time with the value of M. The process loops until M = 0, at which time **not(M=0)** fails and the program is kicked out of the loop.

Elaborate from here and you will soon have a variety of loops for various applications.

Borland is preparing additions to Turbo Prolog, like their various "toolboxes," already out for Turbo Pascal. Thousands of programmers now have Turbo Prolog in hand and are cranking out programs which will soon be appearing on electronic bulletin boards, the national networks, and in the various computer magazines.

It's just starting, you see. The future is declarative programming and Turbo Prolog has us off and running! Go for it!

Appendices

Appendix A

Turbo Prolog 1.1 README File

HERE IS (A SLIGHTLY REFORMATTED VERSION OF) THE LATEST Turbo Prolog README file.

WELCOME TO TURBO PROLOG 1.1

This file contains last-minute information introduced after the manuals were printed. Since this file contains information important to you, please read it in its entirety; it should answer questions you have.

TABLE OF CONTENTS

1. Help

If you have any problems, please read this file and the Manual first. If you still have a question and need assistance, help is available from the following sources:

1. Type GO BORLAND on the CompuServe bulletin board system.
2. Check with your local software dealer or user group.

3. Write to:

    Borland Int'l
    Prolog Tech Support
    4585 Scotts Valley Dr
    Scotts Valley, CA 95066

4. If you have an urgent problem that cannot wait and you have sent in the license agreement from the front of your manual, you may call the Borland Technical Support department. Please be sure to have information about your hardware and DOS version available.

2. Important Information

Library/Samples Disk. The Library disk contains three subdirectories. The subdirectory EXAMPLES contains programs from tutorial portion of the manual; ANSWERS contains possible solutions to the exercises in the manual; and PROGRAMS contains example programs. For a complete file list refer to the section "Files on the Distribution Disks."

Floppy Disk Users Fast Start: Using the Tutorial. First make working copies of your disks; have three disks ready and complete the following in order:

1. Copy Program disk: Put your DOS disk in drive A and a blank disk in drive B, then type:

    ```
    FORMAT B:/S
    ```

    Place the Program disk in drove A and type

    ```
    COPY A:PROLOG.*B:<Enter>
    ```

    Label this disk START-UP disk.

2. Create WORKING disk: Place a blank disk in drive B and type:

    ```
    COPY A:GEOBASE.*B:<Enter>
    ```

    Replace the disk in drive A with the Library disk and type

    ```
    COPY A:\EXAMPLES\*.* B:<Enter>
    ```

    Label this the WORKING disk.

3. Copy Library disk: Place your DOS disk in drive A and a blank disk in drive B, then type:

DISKCOPY A: B:<Enter>

When prompted to do so, place the Library disk in drive A and press <Enter>. This disk will be used later as outlined in the note below.

Run Prolog and try the first example:

1. Put the START-UP disk in drive A and the WORKING disk in drive B, then type:

   PROLOG<Enter>

2. Change the .PRO directory by placing the cursor on Setup and pressing <Enter>, then placing the cursor on Directories and pressing <Enter> twice. Type B:<Enter>.

3. Load the first example by placing the cursor on Files and pressing <Enter>twice. Select EXAMPL01.PRO by placing the cursor on it and pressing <Enter>.

Note: To view the other files contained on the Library disk, follow the process above to copy and load the programs. In step 2 of Using the Tutorial, change the copy command to:

COPY A:\ANSWERS*.* B:<Enter>

if you wish to view the answers to the exercises; or

COPY A:\PROGRAMS*.* B:<Enter>

to view the sample programs.

Creating .EXE Files. When creating .EXE files on a floppy-based system, only the following files should be on the disk in drive A: COMMAND.COM, PROLOG.EXE, PROLOG.OVL, PROLOG.SYS, PROLOG.ERR (optional), PROLOG.HLP (optional), and the source to your program. Drive B should contain PROLOG.LIB and INIT.OBJ only.

Run Prolog from drive A and set both the .OBJ and Turbo directories to B:\. Select .EXE in the Options pull-down menu and select Compile.

If you run out of disk space because your program is large, replace the disk in drive A, *after loading prolog,* with one containing only your source code and PROLOG.OVL. (Prolog remains resident so only PROLOG.OVL is required on disk. See the section "Overlays" below.)

Hard Disk Users Notes. The Library disk contains subdirectories, so to ensure that you copy all the files onto your hard disk, do the following:

1. Create a directory on your hard disk that will contain all the Turbo Prolog files and change to that directory (Chdir).

2. Place the Program disk into drive A and type:

   ```
   COPY A:*.* C:<Enter>
   ```

3. Place the Library disk into drive A

4. Issue the following commands from any DOS prompt:

   ```
   COPY A:*.* C:<Enter>
   COPY A:\EXAMPLES\*.* C:<Enter>
   COPY A:\ANSWERS\*.* C:<Enter>
   COPY A:\PROGRAMS\*.* C:<Enter>
   ```

Overlays. Turbo Prolog is now overlayed in order to include more features without using more RAM. The file PROLOG.EXE is only needed when you first load Turbo Prolog. The overlay file PROLOG.OVL is needed only:

1. During initial start-up of the system.
2. Under the pull-down SETUP.
3. During linking.
4. During the interactive execution of some rarely used routines.

Although PROLOG.OVL is needed when creating an .EXE file, it is not needed when executing an .EXE file.

IBM-CGA. Turbo Prolog is shipped with IBM-CGA "ON," which accommodates systems containing an IBM Color Graphics Adapter or compatible "blinking" video adapter. If you have a video adapter that does not blink or snow (such as Hercules or IBM Enhanced Graphics Adapter), you will want to turn IBM-CGA "OFF." To do so, select Miscellaneous settings from the Setup pull-down menu. Toggle IBM-CGA OFF by pressing <Enter>.

Hex Notation. Hex notation is supported by preceding a number with a dollar sign($). For example, $21 has the decimal integer value of 33.

PROLOG.SYS. Saving and loading .SYS files is done to and from the PRO directory. This allows you to easily have a different .SYS file for every program you develop.

3. Changes to Programs Written in 1.0

Enhancements to Turbo Prolog's heap management requires that you follow the guidelines outlined in the section Programming Style in the manual to assure full use of the heap and avoid error messages 1003 and 1007 (Heap overflow). You will notice that following this style with Version 1.1 gives you much better heap management than Version 1.0.

Equal (=) supports unification of lists, complex structures, and database clauses.

The or (;) is supported within a clause; for example:

```
likes(bill,X) :- likes(tom,X) ; not(likes(sue,X)
```

Characters must be in single quotes; for example, 'a'.

Consult will allow comments and extra lines in a data file.

To use your existing .SYS files with new versions of Turbo Prolog, simply add "V1.10" to the beginning of the .SYS files. For instance, if your existing file looks like:

```
1 0  600 10 10 78 15 26 116 112 . . .
```

add the "V1.10" to the beginning so it will now look like:

```
V1.10 1 0  600 10 10 78 15 26 116 112 . . .
```

You can do this in the Prolog editor.

4. Files on the Distribution Disk

System Disk

README	COM	—	Program you are running.
PROLOG	EXE	—	Compiler
PROLOG	OVL	—	Overlay file needed when starting Prolog and creating .EXE files.
PROLOG	SYS	—	File containing color, window, and directory information
PROLOG	ERR	—	Error messages
PROLOG	HLP	—	Help text

GEOBASE	PRO	—	GeoBase source code.
GEOBASE	INC	—	More GeoBase source code.
GEOBASE	DBA	—	Geography database used by GeoBase.
GEOBASE	HLP	—	Help text for GeoBase.
README		—	This file

Library and Example Programs Disk

PROLOG	LIB	—	Library file needed when linking .OBJ files to create .EXE files.
INIT	OBJ	—	Code required when linking
EXAMPLES		—	Subdirectory containing all the programs used in the Tutorial portion of the manual:
EXAMPLnn	PRO	—	nn is the program number. For instance Program 1 on page 17 of the manual corresponds to EXAMPL01.PRO on disk.
MYPROJ	PRJ	—	Sample Module list from Chap.11, section "Linking Modules."
GLOBDEF	PRO	—	Sample global declarations file for use with MYPROJ.PRJ
MAIN	PRO	—	Main module for use with MYPROJ.PRJ.
SUB1	PRO	—	Submodule for use with MYPROJ.PRJ.
READ64	ME	—	Text file containing information specific to EXAMPLE64.PRO, regarding linking modules from another language to Prolog modules.
EXAMPL65	C	—	Sample C source for EXAMPL64.PRO.
LNKP64	BAT	—	Batch file to link EXAMPL64.OBJ and EXAMPL65.OBJ.
ANSWERS		—	Subdirectory containing answers to the exercises in the manual:
ANSnn	PRO	—	nn corresponds with the page number of the exercise.
DD	DAT	—	Data file used in EX141.PRO.
PROGRAMS		—	Subdirectory containing the following programs:
DIFF	*	—	Example of symbolic differentiation.

D_CURVE	PRO	—	Displays dragon curve.
GENI	*	—	Small example of an expert system shell.
HANOI	PRO	—	Sample program demonstrating a solution to the Towers of Hanoi.
LTEST	PRO	—	Graphics demo.
MENU	PRO	—	General purpose menu system used by GENI and SANAL.
QSORT	PRO	—	Adoption of Clocksin and Mellish quick sort program.
SANAL	*	—	Sentence analyzer.
END			

Appendix B

Delphi Network Sign-Up Information

IF YOU ARE INTERESTED IN JOINING DELPHI TO RETRIEVE THE PAPER on advanced Prolog programming techniques by Michael Covington and for the multitude of other advantages it offers, you may take advantages of the following offer even though you may not be a writer. You also incur no obligation to the Writers Special Interest Group, although you will be welcome to visit at any time.

DELPHI™
WRITERS SPECIAL INTEREST GROUP

*** SPECIAL ON-LINE REGISTRATION ***

We're offering writers and those interested in writing a complimentary lifetime DELPHI membership (a $29.95 value) and a FREE HOUR of connect time (a $7.20 usage credit). Use your free hour at 300, 1200, or 2400 baud during evening, holiday and weekend hours to try the "Writers Special Interest Group" at no risk!

INTRODUCTION

DELPHI, an information service of General Videotext Corporation, now offers the "Writers Special Interest Group," an International Communications Network, open to anyone who writes or is interested in writing. Your personal computer becomes an international information center, allowing you to obtain markets, tips on techniques, and programs of use to writers. Even more exciting, you can have on-line interaction with writers and editors, exchange critiques of your work with fellow writers, post your resume for editors to see, and MUCH more—all from the privacy of your own home.

WHAT YOU NEED TO GET STARTED

Any personal computer and modem can be used, and it's a local call from most areas. DELPHI is easy to use—the commands are simple and straightforward; they're in English. No computer expertise is required. Help is available through our toll-free Customer Service number, 1-800-544-4005.

COMMUNICATE WITH FELLOW WRITERS WORLDWIDE

DELPHI's the "Writers Special Interest Group" is the first and only worldwide communications system to unite all writers and editors. We can be accessed from anywhere in the United States as well as from many other countries including Canada, Japan, Europe, Australia and South America.

ONE SALE CAN PAY FOR MONTHS OF USAGE!

Why limit yourself to weeks old market information? As a member of this network, you'll be able to discuss selling and publishing your work with other writers and editors around the world. There is no better way to share information or search for market and techniques to improve your writing in such a timely or efficient manner. This worldwide service greatly improves your chances of being successful as a writer, and improves the editor's chances of locating you as a contributor to his or her publication.

AN INTERACTIVE BULLETIN BOARD

Our Forum section is an electronic bulletin board that allows users to exchange public messages. You can read messages, add your own messages, or reply to messages posted by other members. Members are encouraged to participate in these discussions which include wide-ranging discussions on techniques, markets, and myriad other things of interest to writers and those interested in writing. Articles, stories, or anything else written by members can be permanently posted in our databases for future reference.

AN INTERNATIONAL CONFERENCE ROOM

Our conference mode allows any number of members to talk to each other "live," just as if we were having a club meeting in the same room! Chat with other writers located thousands of miles away. You can also send private electronic MAIL to any other user and it will be delivered instantly. Using a portable computer, you can even read MAIL and catch up on the latest news from your hotel room!

Here are the Databases that are available for your use:

General Information
Article Advice
Books—Proposals Advice
Critique Exchange
Fiction Advice
News & General Advice
Market Info
Poetry
Resumes
Screen Writing
Writers' Software

LEARN FROM OTHER MEMBERS

No individual can be an expert in all fields of writing and editing, but as a group, we represent a great wealth of knowledge and experience. As we grow, our combined knowledge increases and we create more opportunities for buying and selling our work, so please tell other writers and editors about us whenever possible.

NO SURCHARGE FOR 1200 OR 2400 BAUD USAGE

The "Writers Special Interest Group" is available through the DELPHI Information Service for as little as $6.00 per hour for 300, 1200 or 2400 baud usage during non-business hours, 6 P.M. to 7 A.M. (your local time) on weekdays and all day Saturday, Sunday and selected holidays. You can pay by credit card, Visa, MasterCard or American Express, or by special arrangement, direct billing. There is no minimum monthly charge, so you pay only for what you use. Also, no extra charge for accessing DELPHI through Uninet and Tymnet phone networks.

THE DELPHI ADVANTAGE PLAN

With the DELPHI Advantage, your access rates for using DELPHI can be as low as $6 per hour for the next 12 months!

With the Advantage, you'll begin receiving the latest editions of DELPHI Handbooks and DELPHI Command Cards—absolutely free. You also will receive, free of charge, the DELPHI Oracle newsletter, which announces new services and enhancements to DELPHI and provides you with helpful articles to let you get the most out of DELPHI.

To gain the DELPHI Advantage, just commit to using $24 worth of DELPHI services per month. And that use can be at any time—during either home time or office time. You can sign up for the DELPHI Advantage on-line after you get your regular account.

DELPHI OFFERS EVEN MORE

By signing up for DELPHI, you can also access many other DELPHI features including travel services, airline guides, on-line reference materials including a complete encyclopedia, business and financial information, brokerage services, national news and sports from Associated Press, local and national weather reports, shopping services, appointment schedulers, newsletters, groups & clubs, games and other entertainment features.

TWO MEMBERSHIP OPTIONS FOR NEW USERS

We're offering two membership options:

(a) Sign up for DELPHI now and receive 3 hours ($21.60 usage credit), a DELPHI manual ($19.95), a command card ($2.00) plus your lifetime membership ($29.95), all for the special price of $24.95.

(b) Sign up for DELPHI now and receive a complimentary lifetime membership plus a free hour of connect time (a $7.20 usage credit).

You will be asked a few questions. At each prompt, you can enter a CTRL/Z to start over with the first question, or press CTRL/C to quit entirely. If you have any problems, just call. DELPHI Customer Service can be reached at 1-800-544-4005 or (617) 491-3393 in Mass.

Index

Index

Other Bestsellers From TAB

☐ **EXPERIENCING ARTIFICIAL INTELLIGENCE: An Interactive Approach for the Apple —John J. Morone and Mark R. Hilbush**

Just like having a personal instructor, these disk-based tutorials carry you through the process of learning about artificial intelligence techniques by letting you see and experience them on your Apple screen. To make these books easier to understand, corresponding software has been included with each book. Each disk includes an interactive set of chapters that follow those in the books and clearly illustrates the concepts as they are described. Book plus 3 Disks for Apple *//* with 64K, Apple DOS 3.3 and 80-column card. 192 pp., 116 illus.

Paper/Disk $36.95 **Book No. 2860**

☐ **EXPERIENCING ARTIFICIAL INTELLIGENCE: An Interactive Approach for the IBM® PC —John J. Morone and Mark R. Hilbush**

Just like having your own personal tutor in artificial intelligence (AI) techniques, these disk-based tutorials carry you through the process of learning about AI by letting you see and experience it on your IBM PC screen. To make these books easier to understand, corresponding software has been included with each book. Each disk includes an interactive set of chapters that follow those in the books and clearly illustrates the concepts as they are described. Book plus 2 Disks for IBM PC and Compatibles with 128K and PC-DOS 2.X. 192 pp., 116 illus.

Paper/Disk $29.95 **Book No. 2830**

☐ **DESIGNING AND PROGRAMMING PERSONAL EXPERT SYSTEMS—Carl Townsend and Dennis Feucht**

Discover how new trends in artificial intelligence (AI) concepts can be put to practical use on almost any personal computer including the Apple® II or IBM® PC! Explore expert system programming techniques that can be modified or enhanced to create your own system for electronics, engineering, or other technical applications! It's all here for the taking in this exciting and challenging new sourcebook! 250 pp., 75 illus. (7″ × 10″).

Paper $18.95 **Hard $27.95**
Book No. 2692

☐ **ARTIFICIAL INTELLIGENCE: THEORY, LOGIC AND APPLICATION—James F. Brule**

Explore the leading edge of computer technology . . . probe the outer limits of business productivity offered by today's new-generation microcomputers . . . discover the real-world business applications potential offered by artificial intelligence (AI) techniques! Covers the potentials, the alternatives, and practical advantages and disadvantages of expert systems and AI as business tools. 192 pp., 35 illus. 7″ × 10″.

Paper $12.95 **Hard $18.95**
Book No. 2671

☐ **EXPERT SYSTEMS FOR MICROCOMPUTERS —An Introduction to Artificial Intelligence —Michael Chadwick and John Hannah**

Here, you'll find all the programming techniques needed to put "intelligence" into your microcomputer using BASIC or Logo . . . to create expert system programs that accomplish exactly what you want them to for any business or personal purpose. Leading off with an introduction to expert systems, the authors explain the principles of rule-based systems and demonstrate various procedures designed for many practical applications. 240 pp., 90 illus.

Paper $14.95 **Hard $19.95**
Book No. 2838

☐ **EXPERT SYSTEMS: A Non-Programmers Guide to Development and Applications —Paul Siegel**

This exceptional guide opens the way to a tremendous range of applications for expert systems that you can use in your everyday business. It clarifies how to implement a system, including ways to define problems. You'll learn what an expert system is, methods of thinking that will help you in problem solving, simplified rule language, machine reasoning, and more! 272 pp., 107 illus. 6″ × 9″.

Hard $29.95 **Book No. 2738**

☐ **AN INTRODUCTION TO PROLOG —Ramachandran Bharath, Ph.D.**

This easy-to-follow sourcebook will introduce you to Prolog's different approach to programming called "descriptive" or "declarative" programming. This new style can free you from having to think like a machine to conform to your computer's needs. Instead, it takes over the task of converting your specifications into a form which the computer can execute—and lets you concentrate on the logic of the problem. 224 pp., 100 illus.

Paper $16.95 **Hard $24.95**
Book No. 2682

☐ **LISP—THE LANGUAGE OF ARTIFICIAL INTELLIGENCE—Frederick Holtz**

Now here's your opportunity to learn and use LISP . . . to enter the realm of artificial intelligence with confidence. Holtz explains LISP vocabulary and how artificial intelligence programming concepts differ. You'll get a look at how LISP handles mathematical operations . . . be introduced to logical operators . . . and see how close BASIC input/output is to that of Common LISP. 272 pp., 7″ × 10″.

Paper $16.95 **Hard $21.95**
Book No. 2620